D0722418

Essay Index

New Literary Values

New Literary Values

Studies in Modern Literature

By
David Daiches

Essay Index

Essay Index Reprint Series

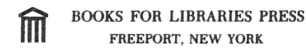

BOOKS FOR LIBRARIES PRESS
FREEPORT, NEW YORK

First Published 1936

Reprinted 1968, 1970
by arrangement with David Daiches and his
literary agents, Harold Ober Associates, Inc.

INTERNATIONAL STANDARD BOOK NUMBER:
0-8369-0358-7

LIBRARY OF CONGRESS CATALOG CARD NUMBER:
68-54342

PRINTED IN THE UNITED STATES OF AMERICA

CONTENTS

INTRODUCTION : ON CRITICISM

I

In an age when more criticism is produced than can be comfortably read or usefully applied, any one who spends his time writing critical essays must be prepared to give a reasoned apologia for his activity. What ought criticism to achieve? Of course its function is to interpret a work of literature to the reader, to help him to understand and appreciate it by examining its nature and exhibiting its merits. But such an answer avoids the real issue. " Merits " can only be recognised as such on a pre-existing standard ; so the critic cannot be content with exhibiting the merits of a work—he must also explain why they are merits, *i.e.* he must reveal his standards. And he must go further : he must *justify* his standards. In other words, before the critic can do any really fruitful work he must make up his mind about the function of literature. The slightest opinion passed upon a work of literature ought to be based on a prior evaluation of literary activity in general ; otherwise the judgment is made, as it were, *in vacuo* and has no real relevance. If we are to attempt to see life whole at all, if we are to make some effort to co-ordinate human activities and processes and reach some kind of equilibrium in our balancing of the diverse forces at work, we must above all aim at making each one of our judgments relevant— relevant to all our other judgments, relevant to life as a whole. The true literary artist, the writer who is concerned with creation only, cannot be aware of the relevance of his work ; for him it fills the whole field of vision and blots out everything else, so that its relation to the rest of human activity is obscured. Such limitation is necessary to the creator but fatal to the critic. The critic must see literature as one of numerous activities, otherwise what function has he at all ? If literature is to be judged by those for whom literature is the whole of life then the creator becomes the best— indeed the only—critic, and criticism becomes mere transcription of the work criticised, ceasing to exist as a separate function. The critic is the link between the work of art and the world, and his duty is to determine their relation. The nature of literary value is dependent on the nature of the relation of art to the whole of life, and to attempt to pass judgment on literature without having come to some conclusion regarding this relation can have no useful result, because it means assessing value on an undetermined criterion.

It may be thought that this is to make too high a claim for criticism, but any activity involving the passing of judgment on products of the human mind will be found on examination to rest on a similar basis. All critical activity is in the nature

of things ultimately philosophical, and to allow
literary criticism alone to take the form of impres-
sionist dilettantism is—to put it no more strongly
—to regard literature as childish trifling, unfit for
serious contemplation. To regard it thus is at least
a logical, if erroneous, point of view ; but to set
a high value on literature and at the same time
refuse to admit that the judging of it is essentially
a philosophical activity, seems to me both illogical
and cowardly. One cannot eat one's cake and
have it. If literature is to be taken seriously and
the immemorial gibe at the poet is to be proved
unwarranted, criticism must take itself seriously too
and concern itself with the nature of literary value.

This is not to say that no criticism is good which
does not take the form of philosophical investigation, but that such investigation must precede any
further discussion. Criticism must assume a stable
standard of values and constant points of reference,
and the discovery of these must be made by each
critic for himself. Otherwise there cannot even be
an intelligent handling of vocabulary. What can
the critic do with such words as " æsthetic,"
" form," " ideal," " significant," unless he has
satisfied himself about their meaning by his own
investigations ? How often do we see quite undefined terms flung about loosely in " critical "
writing which passes for profound ! Definition of
terms is no simple matter ; it is not the beginning
of a thought-process but the end.

Criticism in practice cannot, of course, live up

B

to this ideal. I have tried to indicate its real nature and function by stressing the philosophic aspect, which is so often neglected. It is true that the ideal criticism begins with a philosophic view of life as a whole, proceeds with the separating out of literary activity from human activity in general and the assessing of their mutual relations, deducing from this a norm of literary value, and concludes by the application of this standard to the individual instance. But few critics have the intellectual stamina to go through the whole process, though that need not prevent us from recognising this course as the ideal one to be pursued and basing our own efforts on this recognition. We can attempt to enter the critical field at different stages in the process and, always keeping an undistorted perspective, make in this way some contribution to the whole. But any question we discuss, any judgment we pass or opinion we form, must have reference to the complete process ; it is only by keeping our eye always on the relation of literature to the rest of activity that we can be prevented from lapsing into arid and unprofitable verbosity. Unconscious arguing in a circle is more frequent in all kinds of discussion than most of us realise, and in critical writing it is most frequent of all. It will be easily seen that by viewing all critical thought as part of a process the literary critic can make sure of breaking the circle and producing profitable work.

The difficulties confronting the critic of contemporary writing I have attempted to deal with in a separate essay, *The Judging of Contemporary Literature*. But these difficulties are insignificant compared with those fundamental problems which face the critic of any literature at the very outset. Some are blamed for magnifying those difficulties, some for endeavouring to overcome them by wrong methods. Either of these faults is less than the fault of ignoring them. I cannot claim that in the essays collected here I have finally solved any fundamental critical problem. I have not attempted to work completely through that process which alone will enable the critic to grapple successfully with the chief cruxes of literary criticism. I claim only not to have been insensible of the difficulties of my task, not to have been unaware of the implications involved in any critical judgment. Modern literature presents many interesting phenomena, and it is through a discussion of some of these that I have attempted to make some slight contribution to the under-standing and evaluating of literature.

II

We might approach a discussion of the nature and function of criticism from a different angle. " Literature " and " life " have for long been popularly regarded as constituting two separate categories, the latter being taken to denote the actual everyday experience of men and the former the fantastic imaginings of those who wish to escape from reality. That the separation is false has been recognised by competent critics of every age, but why it is false and the extent to which it is false are more difficult questions. Any value that literature has comes from the nature of its relation to life, to experience—so much is conceded by most, if not by all, critics. A poem like Keats's *Ode to Autumn* is good because it expresses perfectly what does exist, both in its objective aspect, so far as such description can be objective, and in its subjective aspect, *i.e.* the significance of the scene to the beholder. "Expresses perfectly" is, of course, a phrase that needs defining, and I have attempted to do that elsewhere.[1] But what of the matter expressed ? It is something which has " significance," and is therefore " true." A line like

Childe Rowlande to the dark tower came

is also " significant," but not in any ordinary sense true. A romantic critic might say that it possesses " ideal truth " ; it does not record an event which actually took place, but it represents a fundamental human emotion, an aspect of experience we all recognise as genuine, something which does exist, but as a mood, not as an event or a fact. A symbolist critic might praise it as of great symbolic value, refusing, with the inconsistency of his tribe, to identify it with life or actual experience at all. An eighteenth century critic might dismiss it as nonsense, but he would be in a small minority. A

---

[1] *The Place of Meaning in Poetry* (1935).

modern psychological critic might link up its appeal
with some common desire or fear in the subconscious. The point I want to bring out is that
the connection between literature and life, even
when admitted, is very differently explained by
different types of critics. And even those who use
the same terms often use them with different mean-
ings. What do we understand by " significant,"
" ideal truth," etc. ?

Literature is a treatment of experience in
language. Good. Is it, then, the critic's business
to evaluate the experience, or the language, or
both ? They cannot be separated like that, you
say ; language itself is part of experience and
when used as a medium of literary expression
becomes an organic part of the literary work.
Good again. How then do you expect the critic
to set about his business ? Is he primarily an
analyst, taking the work to pieces and examining
the parts, holding every separate part up to the
light and exhibiting it to you ? The fact is that
it matters very much less what method he adopts
in endeavouring to explain and evaluate the work
for the reader than what mental processes he
undergoes himself before he begins to talk at all.
He must allow the work to express itself completely,
to deliver its message and present its case, and then
he must ask himself : " What has this writer done
here ? " There is no need for him to ask also
how he has done it, because the what includes the
how. Literary expression is not so much a matter

of making words express something definite and limited, conceived beforehand, as of trying to make the words say everything at all relevant (or as nearly everything as possible) when they say one given thing, so that form affects content and there is constant tension between the two. If the critic can give an adequate answer to that question "What has the writer done?" he has defined his terms and found his standard of values and can proceed to put pen to paper.

Suppose the critic says : "This author, in feigning a story, has presented significant aspects of human life in an effective manner. He has used his imagination to express something of the truth of experience." The terms that require defining here are "significant," "effective," "imagination," "truth," and perhaps some others. Suppose that he succeeds in defining these terms, concluding that "significant" means "connected with that part of emotional life common to all men"; "effective" means "bringing undimmed to the consciousness of the reader those ideas and emotions which inspired the writer"; "imagination" means "the power to embody and illustrate the general in a particular example"; and "truth" means "the meaning of the fact in terms of human conation, emotion, and sensibility." Before he can estimate the degree to which the author has achieved the aim now defined, he must take the whole of human activity into consideration. Suppose he does this, and arrives at some conclusion on this point also; he has still to satisfy himself regarding the *value* of the writer's achievement ; only a complete metaphysic will enable him to translate this into terms of value. So he turns metaphysician and makes up his mind about literary value. His main work is now done, and he can concern himself with comparing the work with different achievements of the same kind, so as to be able to place it in an order of merit.

I have included this sketch of critical method to show that I am conscious of the difficulties involved in making even the slightest literary judgment, and to enable the reader to see, if he cares, a single thread running through most of the essays. Though they all deal with different topics, most attempt an indirect answer to that question, " What has the writer done ? "—taking the writer discussed as one case of the literary artist in general—and to the other questions included in that. The ultimate question concerns the relation of literature to life, and there are many ways in which one may attempt to answer it. This does not mean that discussions of technical matters cannot constitute criticism, but they are fruitful criticism only when they have reference to this wider question. In fact a simple division of critical writing would be into fruitful and unfruitful. Unfruitful criticism is criticism of separate points in isolation, as though we were to discuss Tennyson's use of vowels without any consciousness of his end in using language as he does, or any assumption of a literary value to which vowel music is subservient. It is not enough to take note of the writer's aim and judge his work by the degree to which he attains it. His aim may not be a literary aim at all, and then no matter how successful he is in achieving it he will not be a great writer. " Romantic " criticism has made a major blunder here. In its natural reaction against " classical " rules and kinds it went to the other extreme and asserted that standards of values varied with the individual instance, and the main duty of the critic was to establish sympathy with the writer. But if there are no ultimate standards applicable equally to Pope and Dante, to Mallarmé and Homer, to Swinburne and Donne, then neither literature nor literary criticism can claim to rank among the major human activities. If literature is a constant and important human activity it is bound to have a highest common factor, and to ignore this factor is to degrade criticism to, at the most, interesting chatter.

" Art for art's sake " is a meaningless slogan because it does not include, or even assume, a definition of art. Naturally every activity of any value is indulged in for its own sake, but the phrase " its own sake " depends for its significance on what that activity is. If art has importance and meaning solely on account of its relation to life (whatever the precise nature of that relation may be) " art's sake " includes " life's sake." By isolating words we do not always isolate ideas. If we say of a nurse that she took up nursing not out of duty or necessity but because she liked " nursing for nursing's sake," we assume that she likes tending the sick, looking after people and helping them to get well, taking pleasure in relieving discomfort and pain. We cannot say that she is not interested in relieving pain, the welfare of her patients does not concern her, because she is concerned only with " nursing for nursing's sake." We cannot isolate the word from the implications of its definition, keeping it as something distinct and self-existent. So with " art," we cannot talk about " art's sake " as implying a distinction between art and life until we have made up our minds whether art means something with a relation to life or not. And if we conclude, as I think we must, that art has value—even existence —because of its relation to life as a whole, then the phrase " art for art's sake " becomes either a truism or an absurdity.

It may be objected that throughout these essays I talk a great deal about literary value, and stress the necessity of defining it, without attempting to define it. It is true that I attempt no direct definition, but I do—I hope—deal with the question indirectly. I have not the temerity to attempt at this stage a complete critique of literature. I can only examine particular instances, making points and raising questions by the way, so that the reader will find the discussions suggestive rather than final. That at least is my aim. And in this rather rambling preface I have endeavoured to supply a background to my later remarks, correcting any superficiality or triviality that may appear there. I am perhaps only providing readers with a stick with which to beat me, for after such a pretentious introduction they may judge the essays by the standards I have indicated for ideal criticism. But the following discussions are " essays " in the strict sense of the word—attempts to treat of some aspects of a given subject. My apologia for criticism has taken the form of an endeavour to define its nature and function ; it is an exposition of the ideal towards which I strive, however far short I may fall in achievement.

III

It is safer to write of ancient than of modern literature. When we are looking back on the past it is so easy to trace movements and see patterns. Time simplifies things so much, neatly dividing human activity into categories and human progress into stages. But simplification always involves some degree of falsification. While it is true that in the present we often cannot see the wood for the trees, looking back on the past we often cannot see the individual trees at all, only the shape of the wood as a whole. Our own age is the only age we can hope really to know and understand. If the same amount of patient investigation which scholars employ in endeavouring to get to know a past age were employed on contemporary events there might be more practical understanding of the conditions under which we live and the forces at work around

us. Contemporary activity is the only activity
really important for us. The past has importance
only in so far as it impinges on the present ; history
has significance primarily because it has brought
about the world we know and live in ; and the
literature of a past age has value for us only because
it still illuminates life as we live it. Literature is
written first for those who are living, who alone
are able to get the maximum amount of meaning
out of it. It is one of the most grievous features of
modern culture that " academic " criticism should
as a matter of course be mostly exercised on past
literature. Past literature is important and often
vital, and the knowledge of it is essential for a
thorough understanding of present work. But no
writer writes primarily for posterity ; he writes for
his own age—he cannot help it, for his own age
conditions his every activity. It is surely a topsy-
turvy state of affairs when the best critical minds of
a generation ignore the work of their contemporaries
and immediate predecessors, turning all their
attention to long-dead authors. Literary activity
is a vital part of life ; no man can live fully without
taking every kind of contemporary activity into
account. Just as contemporary science matters
more to the scientist than the science of previous
ages, and contemporary politics is of more interest
to the politician than the policy of Walpole or the
ideas of the elder Pitt, so contemporary literature
should be of primary importance to the man of
letters. The civilisation of an age consists of many

factors, being made up of $a+b+c+d$ . . . To make for yourself a composite civilisation by taking $a+b+c$ as you find them around you, but ignoring d, substituting d^1, the equivalent from a previous age, is a highly artificial procedure. True, d is conditioned and moulded by d^1 and to some extent contains it in itself, so that a study of d^1 is necessary for a complete understanding of d, as well as being interesting and profitable for its own sake. But that does not mean that a study of d^1 can be a satisfactory substitute for d.

To realise the relation of literature to life is to realise the importance of contemporary literature. Whatever the difficulties in the way of our judging present-day work adequately, it is an essential part of a rounded life to read and appreciate such work. Appreciation is not quite the same as judgment ; the former may be possible under conditions which make the latter difficult. And we should not allow ourselves to be misled by the fact that in an age of transition, such as the present, contemporary literature is difficult both to appreciate and to judge. In the Elizabethan age, in the first half of the eighteenth century, and in the middle of the last century, contemporary literature played a real part in the lives of all educated intelligent people. There was a feeling of reciprocity between author and public which does not exist in a transitional and experimental age. But this reciprocity is a sign of health, it is indicative of the *normality* of literature. Its disappearance, for whatever reason, is to be deplored, and it is the duty of all interested in literature to work for its re-establishment.

So the critic of modern literature has a special function in addition to his general one. His duty is to endeavour to restore that living contact between author and public without which literature cannot play its proper part in contemporary life. It might be argued that a generation which reads and appreciates the literature its own writers produce, even if such literature is subsequently discovered to be of inferior quality, is in a healthier state than the generation which, clinging to its memories of magnificent work done in the past, refuses to have anything to do with contemporary writing. Certainly in the former case literature will be playing the vital part in the life of the people which is its ultimate justification. But on the other hand an acceptance of the new and different as good just because it is new and different is an even more dangerous attitude. The amount of thoroughly bad poetry written to-day in that wilful mood is sufficient warning against holding such a point of view. We must go carefully. Keeping our critical faculties alert, we must be ever on the look-out for falsity and shoddiness in contemporary work, and refuse to acclaim work which we genuinely deem inferior. But on the other hand we must be always willing to learn, always ready to enlarge our sensibility and readjust our attitude in the hope of appreciating what at first sight may seem difficult and wrong-headed. Above all, if we must be ultra-conservative in our literary tastes, let us not be *complacently* so.   It is no virtue to be enthusiastic about every superficial impostor who hides his barrenness under a difficult new style, but it is intellectual cowardice of the worst kind to refuse to make any effort towards an understanding of the new and difficult and to exult in one's inability to understand or appreciate what is really valuable in the modern achievement.

The essays that follow do not deal entirely with living writers, but all the writers dealt with are " modern " in the sense that the problems they faced are still exercising authors to-day.   Katherine Mansfield represents both a new technique and a new sensibility in story telling, and her importance for contemporary writers cannot be over-estimated. Wilfred Owen, too, is important for present-day poets because of his technical achievement as well as his poetic " attitude."   Hopkins I discuss only in his relation to living poets, but even in itself his own work has a modernity too widely recognised to require stressing here.

The first essay stands rather apart : it is concerned largely with poetic technique and does not dwell on deeper issues.   I am aware that different essays may appear to express almost contradictory views.   But I do not think there is any fundamental inconsistency.   A preliminary to a critique of literature, however tentative, must explore many ways if it is not to risk missing the right one.

April, 1936.

GERARD MANLEY HOPKINS AND THE MODERN POETS

THE currents in contemporary poetry are diverse and not always easy to trace. And though the name of Gerard Hopkins has been on the lips of many since Bridges brought out the now famous edition of his poems in 1918, it is not to this one source that we owe the distinguishing features of modern verse. If in the poetry of to-day there is a single highest common factor that can be isolated, that factor consists less of loyalty to any predecessor than of an *attitude*, an attitude to the poetic medium and also an attitude to society. The connection between the technical and social aspects of this attitude may seem remote, and indeed it is remote enough to justify their separate consideration, but an ultimate connection does exist. An attitude to society on the part of a poet involves a definite view of the function of poetry, and a view of the function of poetry is bound to have a reaction on poetic technique ; it is on these lines that a connection can be established between the present-day view of the poetic medium and the contemporary poet's relation to society. But a discussion of the influence of Hopkins must confine itself to the technical aspect only. And perhaps the best way of beginning such a discussion is to pose the simple question : Why is Hopkins involved at all ?

The answer to this question the critics have been inclined to take too much for granted. A poet who sought out new paths as Hopkins did was bound, they assume, to be immediately influential as soon as he became known. But is this true ? If Hopkins had published in his own lifetime would he have influenced the poetry of his contemporaries as he has that of our own generation ? It is very improbable ; but even if we grant that there would have been such influence, the further question remains, which, put in its most extreme form, is just this : Why should a post-war Communist seek inspiration from a nineteenth century Jesuit ? The conditions under which poetry is written to-day are so totally different in every respect from those which prevailed at the time when Hopkins wrote, that the terrific force of the impact of Hopkins' verse on post-war poetry demands an explanation. There is little in the poet's life, in his beliefs, or in his sympathies, to find a response in such a poet as, say, Cecil Day Lewis or Stephen Spender. The answer to our question is not, however, difficult to find : it is simply that the post-war poets, for differing reasons, came to adopt an attitude to the poetic medium which Hopkins, for reasons of his own, had adopted and exploited.

This is the point of contact. Hopkins' use of

language in verse was similar to what the modern poets were demanding and attempting. In their search for models they had gone to poets as different as Donne and Skelton, and still their search was erratic and unfulfilled. Donne, Skelton, Rimbaud, Laforgue, Whitman, as well as the still writing Yeats, Pound and Eliot—it was from these and others that the young poets in the years immediately after the war were seeking inspiration, urged by the new attitude to the poetic medium. But the practice of Hopkins came closest to what they were seeking. Here was one whose attitude to the medium of poetry seemed to be identical with theirs ; and how splendidly he had justified that attitude in practice !

The poetry of Hopkins was made accessible just at the time when English poetry was most sensitive to its influence. It may be that Bridges, appreciative of the atmosphere of his time, published it when he did for that reason : he tells us that his edition was " undertaken in response to a demand that, both in England and America, has gradually grown up from the genuinely poetic interest felt in the poems which I have gradually introduced to the public." Ten years sooner they would have received much less attention—of that there can be little doubt. Ten years later it might have been too late for the influence to be germinal to the extent that it has proved.

What, then, was it in Hopkins' attitude to the poetic medium that appealed so immediately to

the post-war poets ? We have only to listen to the
first two verses of the first of his mature poems to
get a large part of the answer to this question.

> Thou mastering me
> God ! giver of breath and bread ;
> World's strand, sway of the sea ;
> Lord of living and dead ;
> Thou hast bound bones and veins in me, fastened me
> flesh,
> And after it almost unmade, what with dread,
> Thy doing : and dost thou touch me afresh ?
> Over again I feel thy finger and find thee.

> I did say yes
> O at lightning and lashed rod ;
> Thou heardst me truer than tongue confess
> Thy terror,' O Christ, O God ;
> Thou knowest the walls, altar and hour and night ;
> The swoon of a heart that the sweep and hurl of thee trod
> Hard down with a horror of height :
> And the midriff astrain with leaning of, laced with fire of
> stress.

We can see here as well as anywhere in Hopkins
that *straining after a directness beyond that allowed by
the formal syntactic use of language* which was such a
feature of his poetry and which has so appealed to
the poets of our own day. Such poetry is as far
removed from Mallarmé's poetry of suggestion as
it is from Dryden's poetry of statement. There is
here a different directness than that attained by
the directness of " sound-echoing-sense "—even in
its most highly developed form—or of symbolism.
Here was a new way of getting rid of the barrier
that the formal modes of language opposed to the

immediacy of union between subject and object, between the manner of expression and the thing expressed. How much more immediate was the phrase " thou mastering me God ! " than the more conventionally poetic " God who art my master." The poet had leapt at his thought directly, irresistibly, and allowed the form of his expression to be dictated by an emotional rather than a logical sequence. It was this sense of directness that impressed the poets as it impresses any sensitive reader—this and the new rhythms which Hopkins employed. These were the two objects towards which the poets were striving : a new directness and an escape from the normal rhythms of English verse.

The reaction against Victorian poetry in the twentieth century might usefully be compared with the twofold reaction against Spenserian poetry in the beginning of the seventeenth century. Ben Jonson had opposed to Spenser's " romantic " poetic diction a classical economy and cogency of expression, while Donne had revolted from the Petrarchan conceit and the conventional idealisation of love to a full-blooded realistic treatment. Similarly when the Romantic tradition had exhausted itself at the end of the nineteenth century there came on the one hand the direct, forceful, almost epigrammatic poems of A. E. Housman (who, however, stood alone) followed by the quietist poetry of the Georgians, and on the other hand the more " cerebral " and unconventional treatment of Pound and Eliot. It is no accident that Eliot is an admirer of Donne, and that the influence of the greatest of the " metaphysicals " is still strong to-day as in the poetry of Herbert Read, Charles Madge, and others. Donne, in reacting to the poetry of his day, showed the modern poets a way of escape from the nineteenth century and from the Georgians, too. Professor Dover Wilson has recently [1] compared Professor Grierson's edition of Donne to Percy's *Reliques* in its formative influence on a revolutionary school of poetry. The poems of Hopkins are in a similar position. They too helped to give direction to the revolt against the later Romantic tradition in English poetry.

For what were the chief features of late Romantic poetry ? Were they not a desire to use language for the sake of language, a denial of the right of the objective world to influence the medium which described it, the glorification of the means of expression as an end in itself ? Was not this implicit in the work of Tennyson, of Swinburne, and of the poets of the 'nineties ? And it was against this that the poetry of Hopkins was an implied protest. The exploitation of language was no worthy aim in itself : it was the wresting of words to meet fact that mattered. Embroidery was obfuscation—it merely got in the way. Donne and Hopkins were surely agreed on that point,

[1] In his Inaugural Lecture as Professor of Rhetoric and English Literature at Edinburgh University.

and in that they appealed to the moderns. Donne's method of achieving his aim was—if one may be allowed the phrase—to intellectualise his passion ; Hopkins' way was to evolve a practice (and, after the event, a theory) which enabled him to present his feeling and his thought in a progression of highly wrought images and ideas set down in words deliberately chosen for their intensity, their concentration, their approximation, as it were, to the naked fact itself. Is there any poem in the language where the words are so deliberately harnessed to the service of expression as *The Leaden Echo and the Golden Echo*?

How to keep—is there ány any, is there none such, nowhere
    known some, bow or brooch or braid or brace, láce,
    latch or catch or key to keep
Back beauty, keep it, beauty, beauty, beauty, . . . from
    vanishing away ?
Ó is there no frowning of these wrinkles, rankèd wrinkles deep,
Dówn ? no waving off of these most mournful messengers, still
    messengers, sad and stealing messengers of grey ?
No there's none, there's none, O no there's none,
Nor can you long be, what you are now, called fair,
Do what you may do, what, do what you may,
And wisdom is early to despair :
Be beginning ; since, no, nothing can be done
To keep at bay
Age and age's evils, hoar hair,
Ruck and wrinkle, drooping, dying, death's worst, winding
    sheets, tombs and worms and tumbling to decay ;
So be beginning, be beginning to despair.
O there's none ; no no no there's none :
Be beginning to despair, to despair,
Despair, despair, despair, despair.

Here is a use of language at the opposite pole from,

say, that of Swinburne.[1]   With Swinburne language
nearly always came first, and effective language for
its own sake was the aim.   With Hopkins language
was a servant, to be bullied and coerced into as
immediate contact with the thought as was possible.
The rules of grammar and of syntax were not
allowed to stand in the way ; if they affected the
immediacy of the expression they were ignored.
Thus Hopkins sacrificed an obvious intelligibility
to a directness which was not even intelligible—
far less direct—until the meaning had, to use
Hopkins' own term, " exploded."   His obscurity
is due to the fact that his meaning " explodes "
far more rarely than he anticipated.   Naturally
as he knew from the beginning what he wanted to
say, he could not put himself in the place of the
reader, who approached the meaning from the
other end.   A reliance on the eventual " explosion "
of the meaning, rather than on logical exposition
combined with the resources of sound and suggestion, is dangerous, but if it is effective it is much
more direct and powerful and immediate in its
communication than the more normal way.
" Explosion " was often Shakespeare's method,
especially in the later plays.   What does logical
analysis make of this :

> I am question'd by my fears, of what may chance,
> Or breed upon our absence, that may blow
> No sneaping winds at home, to make us say,
> This is put forth too truly,

---

[1] " Words only are only words," wrote Hopkins to
R. W. Dixon, with reference to Swinburne.

or of this :

> The hearts
> That spaniel'd me at heels, to whom I gave
> Their wishes, do discandy, melt their sweets
> On blossoming Cæsar ; and this pine is barkt
> That overtopp'd them all ?

The obscurity here is not so different in kind from that of Hopkins. In both there is the second kind of clearness that Hopkins talks of in a letter to Robert Bridges :

> One of two kinds of clearness one shd. have—whether the meaning to be felt without effort as fast as one reads or else, if dark at first reading, when once made out to *explode*.

A passage from another of Hopkins' letters to Bridges is helpful and relevant here :

> Obscurity I do and will try to avoid so far as is consistent with excellences higher than clearness at first reading.

The trouble, of course, is that Hopkins very often does not achieve that explosive clarity at second reading that he aimed at and to which he sacrificed the " meaning to be felt without effort." And his imitators, not perhaps grasping his principle of explosive meaning at all, fail even more frequently to achieve any kind of intelligibility. What is more distressing, they fail to realise that if you give up surface intelligibility you must submit to the much harder discipline that explosive meaning requires if it is to succeed. Each type of poetry creates its own laws, but they are none the less laws, and success is impossible if they are not respected. The poetry of Hopkins is highly disciplined—over-disciplined, some may maintain, but no one can deny that his finest poems are due to a wrestling with language which did not come easily however spontaneous the effect may be to the reader. It was, then, his impatience with the poetic medium as generally accepted in the nineteenth century that brought Hopkins into immediate contact with the modern poets. The practice in which such impatience resulted was rationalised in his theory of " Sprung Rhythm," a theory highly important in its liberating effect on English metre since 1918.

Why do I employ sprung rhythm at all ? (Hopkins wrote to Bridges in 1877)—Because it is the nearest to the rhythm of prose, that is the native and natural rhythm of speech, the least forced, the most rhetorical and emphatic of all possible rhythms, combining, as it seems to me, opposite and, one would have thought, incompatible excellences, markedness of rhythm—that is rhythm's self—and naturalness of expression —for why, if it is possible in prose to say " lashed rod," am I obliged to weaken this in verse, which ought to be stronger, not weaker, into " láshed birch-ród " or something ?

The briefest adequate explanation of sprung rhythm is given by Hopkins himself in a letter to R. W. Dixon :

To speak shortly, it consists in scanning by accents or stresses alone, without any account of the number of syllables, so that a foot may be one strong syllable or it may be many light and one strong. I do not say the idea is altogether new ; there are hints of it in music, in nursery rhymes and popular jingles, in the poets themselves, and, since then, I have seen it talked about as a thing possible in critics. Here are instances—" Díng, dóng, béll ; Pússy's ín the wéll ; Whó pút her ín ? Líttle Jóhnny Thín. Whó púlled her óut ? Líttle Jóhnny Stóut." For if each line has three stresses or three feet it follows that some of the feet are of one syllable only. So too " Óne, twó, Búckle my shóe " passim. In Campbell you have " Ánd their fléet alóng the déep próudly shóne "— " Ít was tén of Ápril mórn bý the chíme," etc. ; in Shakspere " Whý shd. thís désert bé ? " corrected wrongly by the editors ; in Moore a little melody I cannot quote ; etc. But no one has professedly used it and made it the principle throughout, that I know of. Nevertheless to me it appears, I own, to be a better and more natural principle than the ordinary system, much more flexible, and capable of much greater effects. . . . Also I have written some sonnets and a few other little things ; some in sprung rhythm, with various other experiments—as " outriding feet," that is parts of which do not count in the scanning (such as you find in Shakspere's later plays, but as a licence, whereas mine are rather calculated effects) ; others in the ordinary scanning counterpointed (this is counterpoint : " Hóme to his móther's hóuse prívate retúrned " and " Bút to vánquish by wísdom héllish wíles " etc.) ; others, one or two, in common uncounterpointed rhythm.

He goes on to say that

Milton is the great standard in the use of counterpoint. In Paradise Lost and Regained, in the last more freely, it being an advance in his art, he employs counterpoint more or less everywhere, markedly now and then ; but the choruses of Samson Agonistes are in my judgment counterpointed throughout ; that is, each line (or nearly so) has two different coexisting scansions. But when you reach that point the secondary or " mounted rhythm," which is necessarily a sprung rhythm, overpowers the original or conventional one and then this becomes superfluous and may be got rid of ; by taking that last step you reach simple sprung rhythm. Milton must have known this but had reasons for not taking it.

We come across passages of this kind frequently throughout the letters of Hopkins to Bridges and R. W. Dixon, and they show what an indefatigable metrical theorist he was. All his life Hopkins was interested in the theory of metre, classical even more than English, and it is important to bear this in mind when comparing his work with that of his modern imitators. The difference in quality as regards metrical achievement is often explained by the fact that Hopkins had studied the subject carefully in all its aspects and came to the writing of poetry with a technical knowledge which none of the modern poets possesses. This does not, however, prevent us from realising that Hopkins' elaborate theory of sprung rhythm—and he has a lot more to say than in the extract quoted—was a rationalisation of an instinctive desire to achieve more direct methods of expression in more spontaneous-sounding rhythms.

Hopkins had other peculiarities. His use of tmesis, enjambement, and coined words are three of the more important. He made frequent and often subtle use of alliteration, too, and a less frequent though equally noticeable use of peculiar rhymes, rhymes which often strike the reader as ludicrous, such as " crew in " with " ruin," " boon he on " with " communion," and " Irish " with " sire he sh(ares)," " shares " being the first word of the third line, and the line being " rove over." All these features sprang from the same cause— impatience with the syntactical division of language

into ordered components and a desire to get behind
syntax to a more cogent logic. Perhaps in less
than half of his work can he be called successful
in this effort, but had he lived he would probably
have achieved a more uniformly successful method
of attaining his aims—aims which, let it be repeated,
he so largely shares with the modern poets.

When Hopkins is successful he attains a rhythmic
and musical effect which is integral to the verse in a
peculiar degree ; it is not in any way superimposed
on the meaning. The *Echoes* song is a fine example
of this, as is also the famous *Windhover* :

I caught this morning morning's minion, king-
    dom of day light's dauphin, dapple-dawn-drawn Falcon,
        in his riding
Of the rolling level underneath him steady air, and striding
High there, how he rung upon the rein of a wimpling wing
In his ecstasy ! then off, off forth on swing,
    As a skate's heel sweeps smooth on a bow-bend : the hurl
        and gliding
Rebuffed the big wind.   My heart in hiding
Stirred for a bird,—the achieve of, the mastery of the thing !

But the dangers of this method are easily shown :

To what serves mortal beauty—dangerous ; does set danc-
ing blood—the O-seal-that-so feature, flung prouder form
Than Purcell tune lets tread to ?

Here there is no white-hot welding of form and
content, but only a painful stuttering.   When a
passion which is single struggles with a medium
that consists of separate words a fusion must take
place or the words scatter to the ground ineffective.
At his best Hopkins does achieve this fusion.   Perhaps

no poet after Shakespeare shows such a sense of the infinite gap between emotion which is single and unified, and the medium of language which has to be assembled in time before the emotion can be expressed. Other poets showed no concern when faced with this fact, accepting the medium as it was and making the best of it. Only Shakespeare, with a technique that in the last resort defies analysis, was able to bridge that gap consistently. It is Hopkins' greatness that, in his own way, he also did so—occasionally. It would be idle to maintain that he did so often.

The publication of Hopkins, and the discovery by the modern poets that he had had a problem similar to their own resulting in an attitude to the poetic medium similar to their own, led at once to imitation of every kind. The imitation, which consisted in superimposing crude Hopkinsesque fragments on to an alien style, was of no value and only did harm, but the influence was also felt in a more valuable way than that. The poets absorbed the rhythms of Hopkins and these helped to loosen up their style, to redeem it on the one hand from sloppy poetic prose and on the other from congested and unpoetic " wit-writing." The use a poet made of the example of Hopkins was a very good test of his understanding of Hopkins' achievement. The poet who made the example an excuse to write insensitively and obscurely was modelling his verse on Hopkins' failures.

Once we see Hopkins as a rallying point after

years of experiment with the poetic medium we can attempt to consider his influence on the moderns in some detail. The work of Auden, Spender, and Day Lewis gives us examples of the influence used to loosen up the rhythm and the form of expression in a verse whose texture is much less highly wrought than that of Hopkins.

> Me, March, you do with your movements master and rock
> With ring-whirl, whale-wallow, silent budding of cell . . .

That is Auden. The opening of Day Lewis's *Magnetic Mountain* is Hopkins' *Windhover* subdued, tamed, with none of the superb movement of the original, but none the less effective :

> Now to be with you, elate, unshared,
> My kestrel joy, O hoverer in wind,
> Over the quarry furiously at rest
> Chaired on shoulders of shouting wind.
>
> Where's that unique one, wind and wing married,
> Aloft in contact of earth and ether ;
> Feathery my comet, Oh too often
> From heav'n harried by carrion cares.

We find the rhythms of Hopkins reproduced fairly closely in a recent poem of T. H. White, *A Dray Horse* :

> Meek Hercules, passion of arched power bowed to titanic affection ;
> Docile though vanquishing, stout-limber in vastness, plunging and spurning thy road ;
> Taughten thy traces, triumph past me, take thy shattering direction
> Through misty Glasgow, dragging in a tremendous beer-wagon thy cobble-thundering load.

There are many such examples.   More difficult
to discover at a first reading are subtler parallels,
echoes of cadences and of typical phrases.   The
last two lines of the first verse of Hopkins' poem on
Purcell run :

An age is now since passed, since parted ; with the reversal
Of the outward sentence low lays him, listed to a heresy, here.

Compare with that the concluding lines of one of
Auden's poems :

> The hard bitch and the riding-master,
> Stiff underground ; deep in clear lake
> The lolling bridegroom, beautiful, there.

" Low lays him, listed to a heresy, here " : " The
lolling bridegroom, beautiful, there."   In both we
have the same cadence, a cadence very rare in
English poetry.   The sequence :   noun, paren-
thetical adjectival phrase, emphatic adverb, is
fairly frequent in Hopkins and offers new oppor-
tunities for emotional statement.

Hopkins' frequent omission of the relative pronoun
—a feature which Bridges noted as contributing to
obscurity—is imitated more by Day Lewis than by
any other modern poet.   A line like

> Hidden the mountain was to steel our hearts

is ambiguous because of such omission.   A less
ambiguous example is

> Shallowly breathes the wind or holds his breath,
> As in ambush waiting to leap at convoy
> Must pass this way.

Day Lewis, too, sometimes makes use of distinctive Hopkins' features of a less easily definable nature :

> Beauty breaks ground, O, in strange places.
> Seen after cloudburst down the bone-dry watercourses,
> In Texas a great gusher, a grain-
> Elevator in the Ukraine plain ;
> To a new generation turns new faces.

Here we have Hopkins' habit of inserting the exclamation medially and his splitting a word at the end of a line for the rhyme, as well as a general feel of Hopkins in the verse.

It is curious that no modern poet seems to have profited by Hopkins' rare but perfect use of three-stressed couplets, where a new and individual cadence is given to a metrical form which, in any other hands, might have been too reminiscent of Prior's octo-syllables. There is, for example, that perfect piece *Spring and Fall : to a young child.*

> Márgarét, áre you grieving
> Over Goldengrove unleaving ?
> Léaves, líke the things of man, you
> With your fresh thoughts care for, can you ?
> Áh ! ás the heart grows older
> It will come to such sights colder
> By and by, nor spare a sigh
> Though worlds of wanwood leafmeal lie ;
> And yet you will weep and know why.
> Now no matter, child, the name :
> Sórrow's springs áre the same.
> Nor mouth had, no nor mind, expressed
> What heart heard of, ghost guessed :
> It ís the blight man was born for,
> It is Margaret you mourn for.

The beauty and originality of this simple-seeming
metre can best be shown by putting it beside
Prior's octo-syllables :

> What nymph should I admire, or trust
> But Cloe beauteous, Cloe just ?
> What nymph should I desire to see
> But her who leaves the plain for me ?
> To whom should I compose the lay,
> But her who listens when I play ?
> To whom, in song, repeat my cares,
> But her who in my sorrow shares ?
> For whom should I the garland make,
> But her who joys the gift to take,
> And boasts she wears it for my sake ?
> In love am I not fully blest ?
> Lisetta, pr'ythee tell the rest.

Yet modern poets have not taken it up. They
have preferred to go to Skelton for their short
lines. Here, for example, is a typical short-line
passage from Auden :

> Sitting all day
> By the open window
> Say what they say
> Know what to know
> Who brought and taught
> Unusual images
> And new tunes to old cottages,
> With so much done
> Without a thought
> Of the anonymous lampoon
> The cellar counterplot,
> Though in the night
> Pursued by eaters
> They clutch at gaiters

> That straddle and deny
> Escape that way,
> Though in the night
> Is waking fright,

which seems to echo Skelton directly :

> Her beauty to augment
> Dame Nature hath her lent
> A wart upon her cheek,—
> Who so list to seek
> In her visage a scar,—
> That seemeth from afar
> Like to a radiant star,
> All with favour fret,
> So properly it is set !
> She is the violet,
> The daisy delectable,
> The columbine commendable,
> The jelofer amiable :
> For this most goodly flower,
> This blossom of fresh colour,
> So Juppiter me succour,
> She flourisheth new and new
> In beauty and virtue . . .

The influence of Skelton is everywhere in modern poetry, and is not confined to Robert Graves.

But to return to Hopkins. For all the influence which he has had on the modern poets, there is a fundamental difference between his work and that of his imitators—even technically. In the first place, none of the moderns have the tactual and visual sense that Hopkins had ; their verse is more purely intellectual. Hopkins' imagination was to a very high degree sensuous, and the difficulty of his poems is often due less to intellectual subtlety

F

than to the welding of different kinds of sensuous experience in a struggle for complete expression. Edith Sitwell does the same sort of thing much more blatantly when she talks of the " purring sound of fires," the " dark songs of birds," the " blue wind," the " creaking light," etc. Hopkins' confusion of the senses is less obvious and based more on a preternatural sensitivity than on a desire to be effective. In his sonnet *Duns Scotus's Oxford* we see how the senses of sight and hearing determine the vocabulary :

Towering city and branchy between towers ;
Cuckoo-echoing, bell-swarmèd, lark-charmèd, rook-raked,
    river-rou'nded ;
The dapple-eared lily below thee ; that country and town did
Once encounter in, here coped and poised powers.

None of the moderns have this sensuous awareness. Spender, for example, writes :

My parents kept me from children who were rough
And who threw words like stones and who wore torn clothes.
Their thighs showed through rags. They ran in the street
And climbed cliffs and stripped by the country streams.

There is a purely intellectual quality here that Hopkins, for all the " cerebration " in his verse, would never have allowed. The meaning is conveyed by verbs which convey nothing to the senses. " Their thighs *showed* through rags." " Who wore torn clothes." Hopkins would never have been satisfied with the abstract verb " showed " or the general phrase " wore torn clothes " : he would have made you see them instead of merely talking about them. Hopkins stands alone in the intensity of his perceptions, and this involves an important difference in his use of the poetic medium.

Hopkins, too, had a gift for naturalising words in foreign contexts which the modern poets have only partly inherited. In a phrase like " What lovely behaviour of silk-sack clouds " (from *Hurrahing in Harvest*) the word " behaviour " is surprising and effective. This device, when it is found in modern poetry, has none of the subtlety with which Hopkins used it.

But there are more important differences than these between the poetry of Hopkins and that of contemporary poets. The main one is this. Hopkins was sure of the content, the matter, of his verse ; he had no problem there—he took it for granted that the kind of subject he wished to write about was a fit subject for poetry and he wrote only when the inspiration came. All his conscious attention was devoted to form. His experiments and innovations were all due to a striving after new means of expression, not after new matter to express. The new matter he may have had, but it came without striving, and his desire to justify his themes theologically had no relevance to his poetic activity. As a poet he was concerned with originating a new technique, and it was to this that all his conscious experimentation was directed. But his modern imitators are even more preoccupied with content than with form. Indeed it may be questioned whether they are fundamentally concerned about form at all. When we see how unscrupulous a poet like Auden can be in using trivial and unworthy forms in order to ensure that a certain point will be " got across " to a certain audience, when we see him and others taking advantage of every meretricious trick available in order to achieve a purpose which is not poetic at all, we begin to wonder how far the poets of to-day are concerned to write *good* as distinct from temporarily *effective* poetry. Many of them have adopted sprung rhythm ready-made without any understanding of its organic nature or appreciation of its οἰκείη ἡδονή, its peculiar pleasure. In technique their only concern seems to be towards a looseness *ad infinitum*, counterbalanced, when they remember, with a stiffening of intricacy by some such method as the Wilfred Owen type of assonance. And all the while they grow more and more concerned about their subject, what they are to write about. This was not Hopkins' attitude, and it puts a big gulf between his poetry and that of his modern imitators.

So while Hopkins and the modern poets have similar attitudes to the poetic medium, they differ in their more fundamental attitudes to poetry. To Hopkins, an attitude to the medium was identified with a complete theory of poetry—at least the other elements in the theory were obvious and taken as a matter of course.[1] If you had some-

---

[1] *Cf.* his " Canons of Poetry " in a letter to R. W. Dixon, 14th April 1884. They all deal with technical questions.

thing to put into poetry and came seriously to your subject, that was all that mattered. " A kind of touchstone of the highest or most living art," he wrote Bridges in 1886, " is seriousness ; not gravity but the being in earnest with your subject— reality." He was not worried about what the poet *ought* to say—as long as he meant what he did say. The matter for poetry was not itself poetry : the way the matter was used was what made poetry. He wrote to Bridges of the Irish that " they always mistake the matter of poetry for poetry." The modern poets have not yet decided on what the matter of poetry is, though they seem to have reached some agreement on what it is not. The reasons for this state of affairs in modern poetry cannot be discussed in such a sketch as this ; it would require a closer study of contemporary literature and society than is possible here. Here the fact can only be noted, and stressed as an important point of difference between Hopkins and his followers.

A less fundamental but equally interesting point of difference is that Hopkins did not allow his preoccupation with technique to interfere with his lyrical faculty—he retained the ability to *sing*, which the modern poets have lost through over much self-consciousness. The self-consciousness of the modern poet is twofold : he has too much knowledge of the psychology of poetic creation, of his own mental processes, to be comfortable in creation, and, secondly, an undue social sensitiveness makes him worried and apologetic in his artistic activity. Hopkins suffered from neither of these ills, and that was his good fortune rather than his merit : had he lived to-day he could hardly have avoided the influence of modern psychology or the effects of an altered social atmosphere. But as things were he retained a remarkably fresh lyrical vein.

> Look at the stars ! look, look up at the skies !
> O look at all the fire-folk sitting in the air !

There is nothing like this in contemporary poetry—nothing, either, like the more meditative mood of *God's Grandeur* and *The Sea and the Skylark*, which show a restrained lyrical quality rare in any poet. This lyrical faculty of Hopkins is akin to that startling directness of approach which produces some of his most effective lines :

> The Eurydice—it concerned thee, O Lord,

or

> And you were a liar, O blue March day.

The verse of the contemporary poets is technically much simpler and more elementary than that of Hopkins. Auden and Spender, for example, though they show considerable Hopkins influence, generally use loose iambic feet with simple counterpoint and equivalence which gives something of the effect of sprung rhythm without being so technically accomplished or so highly wrought. This is the third major difference between Hopkins and his imitators.

For all his influence on the run and feel of the lines in modern poetry, Hopkins does not seem to have had as much influence on details of arrangement and structure as another poet whom both poets and critics of to-day seem very reluctant to mention : I mean Walt Whitman. To any one who comes to contemporary verse after reading Whitman the influence seems obvious and overwhelming. Why the poets are reluctant to admit, and the critics slow to detect, influence is difficult to tell ; certainly it seems more fashionable to hold up Hopkins as the sole model. The influence of Hopkins, as has already been shown, is undoubtedly great, but that is no reason why Whitman should be denied his share.

To the drum-taps prompt
The young men falling in and arming,
The mechanics arming, (the trowel, the jack-plane, the black-
    smith's hammer, tost aside with precipitation),
The lawyer leaving his office and arming, the judge leaving the
    court . . .

Is not that passage from Whitman akin to this, from Spender :

From all these events, from the slump, from the war, from
    the boom,
From the Italian holiday, from the skirring
Of the revolving light for an adventurer,
From the crowds in the square at dusk, from the shooting,
From the living, from the dying, however we prosper in
    death . . . ?

And this from Day Lewis has a similar movement :

The man with his tongue in his cheek, the woman
With her heart in the wrong place, unhandsome, unwholesome;
Have exposed the new-born to worse than weather,
Exiled the honest and sacked the seer.

Yet these are examples picked out quite at random. In the works of Auden, also, we often find the movement of the verse very reminiscent of Whitman. Perhaps, too, the comrade *motif* in the work of Auden, Spender, and Day Lewis, that stress on the " palpable and obvious love of man for man " which Day Lewis affirms to be one of the keynotes of modern poetry in his essay *A Hope for Poetry*—perhaps this draws some inspiration from Whitman's *Calamus* with its constant stressing of the love of comrade for comrade, its almost hysterical idealisation of friendship. There is, too, a similarity between Whitman's realism and familiarity, introduced deliberately into the highest themes, and the treatment of such themes in contemporary verse. It is perhaps significant that three lines from Whitman stand as the motto to part two of *Transitional Poem*, while a line from Hopkins stands at the head of the last section of *The Magnetic Mountain*.[1]

There is a poet whose influence on modern

[1] Perhaps, too, Hopkins' verdict on Whitman has significance. He wrote to Bridges in 1882 : " I always knew in my heart Walt Whitman's mind to be more like my own than any other man's living. As he is a very great scoundrel, this is not a pleasant confession."

poetry would undoubtedly have been greater had Hopkins not appeared to divert the current in his own direction ; this is Wilfred Owen. Owen had his own problems to solve in connection with the poetic medium, and he solved them in a way of his own. He was less revolutionary in his method but quite as effective. Besides his powerful and restrained use of traditional forms, as in his sonnet *Anthem for Doomed Youth*, he had a freer method of expression where the movement of lines is supple yet firmly controlled. Such a poem as *The Send-off* shows a sureness of touch and a control over the medium that Hopkins often lacked. It might have been a good thing if Owen, rather than Hopkins, had become the model for modern poets. Hopkins' style was too individual, too much the solution of a personal difficulty, to be used with real success by imitators ; the style of Owen is more adaptable to wise imitation.

Owen is recognised by the poets themselves as an influence on their poetry. Day Lewis places him beside Hopkins and Eliot as one of the three great forces. But, though all pay lip service to him, he was too conservative in his use of the medium to have profound influence in our restless age. His peculiar use of assonance is the one feature of his style which has been generally imitated. His matching of " birds " with " bards," " leaves " with " lives," " death " with " dearth," " smile " with " small " and similar half-rhymes (of course it is not strictly assonance at all, but

G

deliberate dissonance) is imitated frequently by
Auden :

> Since you are going to begin to-day
> Let us consider what it is you do.
> You are the one whose part it is to lean,
> For whom it is not good to be alone.
> Laugh warmly, turning shyly in the hall
> Or climb with bare knees the volcanic hill, etc.

Apart from the imitation of this minor technical
device, Owen has been left alone by the poets of
to-day, though they all profess admiration for him.

Another poet who has been going his own way
amid all the fuss is Roy Campbell, whose rich
sounding descriptive verse and Popeian satire stand
very much apart from the rest of contemporary
poetry. Spender, however, seems to catch his tones
occasionally, and his poem on *Beethoven's Death
Mask* is quite in Campbell's descriptive manner :

> I see the thick hands clasped ; the scare-crow coat ;
> The light strike upwards at the holes for eyes ;
> The beast squat in that mouth, whose opening is
> The hollow opening of an organ pipe :
> There the wind sings and the harsh longing cries.

Again, we might claim that had Hopkins not
appeared Campbell would be a more heeded poet
than to-day he is. Of his genuine poetical ability
there can be no question.

Tracing the disintegration of the traditional
English poetic medium through Whitman, Pound
and Eliot, we can readily see how Hopkins stepped
in to play at once a constructive and destructive

rôle—constructive in that he did achieve a valuable new metric (not altogether new, but at least revived), destructive, in that his impatience with the formal limitations of language coincided with a similar impatience on the part of the post-war poets and encouraged them to go to strange lengths in their desire for immediacy of expression. His total influence on modern poetry cannot yet be estimated. It is still difficult to see clearly into the tangle of influences which have been working on English poetry during the last decade, and which are still potent. What is due to Donne and Eliot, what to Pound, what to Hopkins, what to Whitman, what to Yeats, and what to the French poets at the end of the last century and later—to mention only some of the forces at work—cannot yet be decided. But however we may apportion the influence, we cannot doubt that Hopkins did do much, and for the reason that he represented a definite step in the disintegration of the traditional medium. What that disintegration is to lead to, what the goal is towards which this line of development is tending, we cannot at present tell. We can only try to keep in touch with all developments as they occur, to understand them by endeavouring to determine their sources and *raison d'être*, and to assess their value as poetry with the help of clear notions about the nature of poetry. That, perhaps, is the whole duty of the present-day student of literature towards contemporary verse. It certainly is not less.

January, 1936.

THE POETRY OF WILFRED OWEN

Nevertheless, except you share
  With them in hell the sorrowful dark of hell,
  Whose world is but the trembling of a flare,
  And heaven but as the highway for a shell,

You shall not hear their mirth :
  You shall not come to think them well content
  By any jest of mine. These men are worth
  Your tears : you are not worth their merriment.
                        (*Apologia pro Poemate Meo.*)

IT seems presumption for one who did not grow
up till after the war was over to write of the poetry
of Wilfred Owen ; yet it is not really so. Really
it is a tribute to the greatness of his work that it
can be critically discussed by a generation that
was too young to appreciate the realities of war.
Unlike most war poetry, Owen's does not belong
to a single period, it does not derive its value solely
from the background of special emotion against
which it was originally set. His genius had not
only a universalising quality, but a quality of
insight and penetration that enabled him to pierce
to the heart of phenomena by stating them, recording them. His mood was foreign alike to purposeless
bitterness and uncontrolled sentimentality. He had
something to say, and he said it effectively, poetic-
ally, so that eighteen years after the end of the

war—eighteen years after Owen's own death, which took place a week before the Armistice—his reputation is greater than ever, and the power and cogency of what he has written remains, as it will always remain.

Like so many young poets, Owen began in the Keats tradition. He loved language and played excitedly with its riches. There is more than a superficial parallel between the pre-war Owen and the immature Keats, while the change wrought in Owen by the war can be compared to the change that took place in Keats with the consciousness that he had only a limited time to live. Keats' development is illustrated most clearly in his letters, but the wisdom and maturity that came to Owen with the war is patent in his poems. What Mr Blunden has called " the ' Endymion ' phase of Owen's poetical life " came abruptly to a close ; the early Keats and the more superficial side of Tennyson vanished from his work ; the pleasant dream-like note of

> Leaves
> Murmuring by myriads in the shimmering trees

together with the sensuous quality of

> Fleshes
> Gleaming with wetness to the morning gold

(from the same poem) gave place to a clear-eyed awareness and a sense of reality (reality of fact and also reality of values) that sometimes startle us,

as the greatest touches of the greatest poets startle
us by their truth.

It is interesting to note the two alternative endings
to an early sonnet (1910) given by Mr Blunden in
the memoir prefixed to his edition of the poems :

> Yet shall Keats' voice sing on and never tire

is the first alternative, and the second,

> Yet shall I see fair Keats, and hear his lyre.

Here we see two opposite faults of immaturity.
The first line stumbles with its consonants (" Keats'
voice sing ") and is hard to read, while the second,
flowing enough in sound and movement, is vitiated
by padding and a too conventional romantic vocabulary ("*fair* Keats " ; " hear his *lyre* "). This is
the early Owen, writing in an already worn
tradition, but kept vital by his poetical curiosity
and his experiments in verbal technique. His war
poetry shows an amazing advance in expression as
well as content.

In his sketch of a Preface, Owen wrote : " Above
all I am not concerned with Poetry. My subject
is War and the pity of War. The Poetry is in the
pity." Of course he was concerned with poetry—
his whole life proclaims that—but we know what
he meant. He was not concerned to decorate
fact, to poetise experience for the sake of poetry,
to make life an excuse for a theme. He wrote
poetry for the sake of life, in order to reach out
through the facts of war to fundamental aspects

of human thought and emotion. He taught as he learnt :

> But the old Happiness is unreturning.
> Boys' griefs are not so grievous as youth's yearning,
> Boys have no sadness sadder than our hope.
> We who have seen the gods' kaleidoscope,
> And played with human passions for our toys,
> We know men suffer chiefly by their joys.

It is this ability to accept the lesson and convey it simply (yet with great art) that distinguishes Owen from most other war poets. He kept himself in control, kept his vision undistorted by blind anger or unreasoning despair. Sassoon, for example, often takes the line of least resistance in his war poetry and spoils his work by a flood of particular emotion, or undue irony, obviously distorting the essential truth of the situation in order to find a vent for this emotion. When describing a war-time music-hall show, with chorus girls singing about the Kaiser and the Tanks, he concludes :

> I'd like to see a Tank come down the stalls,
> Lurching to rag-time tunes, or " Home, sweet Home "—
> And there'd be no more jokes in music-halls
> To mock the riddled corpses round Bapaume.

The fact is, of course, that the jokes are *not* mocking the riddled corpses round Bapaume ; they are just an attempt at temporary escape from unpleasant reality, and to regard them as Sassoon does in this poem shows a distortion, however unconscious, due to a morbidly aggravated sensitivity. Owen sees into things with more genuine vision. His sense of the

futility of war is no less than Sassoon's, but he
expresses it with greater restraint and, therefore,
more effectiveness. In his short poem *Futility* he is
talking of a smashed-up soldier : " Move him into
the sun," he says—

> If anything might rouse him now
> The kind old sun will know.
>
> Think how it wakes the seeds,—
> Woke, once, the clays of a cold star.
> Are limbs, so dear-achieved, are sides,
> Full-nerved—still warm—too hard to stir ?
> Was it for this the clay grew tall ?
> —O what made fatuous sunbeams toil
> To break earth's sleep at all ?

This is real pathos, genuine emotion with the facts
undistorted. It can be put beside other of his lines,
like

> The pallor of girls' brows shall be their pall ;
> Their flowers the tenderness of silent minds,
> And each slow dusk a drawing-down of blinds,

to show what Owen meant when he wrote : " All
a poet can do to-day is to warn. That is why the
true Poets must be truthful." He did not sacrifice
truth to indignation. Even in that terrible poem
Disabled there is no distortion :

> Once he liked a blood-smear down his leg,
>   After the matches, carried shoulder-high.
> It was after football, when he'd drunk a peg,
>   He thought he'd better join.—He wonders why.
> Someone had said he'd look a god in kilts,
>   That's why ; and maybe, too, to please his Meg ;
> Aye, that was it, to please the giddy jilts
>   He asked to join. He didn't have to beg ;

> Smiling they wrote his lie ; aged nineteen years.
>   Germans he scarcely thought of ; all their guilt,
> And Austria's, did not move him.   And no fears
>   Of Fear came yet.   He thought of jewelled hilts
> For daggers in plaid socks. . . . .

The plain facts, but how much heightened by the previous lines :

> Now he will never feel again how slim
> Girls' waists are, or how warm their subtle hands ;
> All of them touch him like some queer disease.

It is by effective juxtaposition and arrangement that Owen gives greatness to his poems, not by wresting and elaborating the single fact out of all relation to truth under the impulse of an uncontrollable emotion.   Owen could not write, like Sassoon :

> " He's a cheery old card," grunted Harry to Jack
> As they slogged up to Arras with rifle and pack.
>   .   .   .   .   .   .
> But he did for them both by his plan of attack.

This is obvious distortion to make a point.   The general's plan of attack did not bear the simple causal relation to the death of the two soldiers that Sassoon indicates.   There is enough real irony in war to make such subterfuges unnecessary, though it is much more difficult—the line of *most* resistance —to make poetry out of the genuine fact.   Owen does it in *Dulce et Decorum Est* and *Mental Cases* and half-a-dozen other poems.

" All a poet can do to-day is warn.   That is why

H

the true Poets must be truthful." But there are
many kinds of truth. Obvious truth of fact—truth
to what he *saw*—is not the easiest to tell, but Owen
told it, holding it in his hand, as it were, unbroken,
and displaying it to all who wished to see. He
captured, too, another kind of truth—truth to
what he *felt*. That this was worth recording was
due to the fineness of Owen's own character,
which guaranteed a value to his sense of things
greater than that which belonged to the things
themselves. Here was no distortion to meet emotion,
but interpretation to explain an urgent sense of
significance. *Strange Meeting* is a poem of this
kind. He tells how in a vision he escaped out of
battle " down some profound dull tunnel " to meet
a strange face :

> " Strange friend," I said, " here is no cause to mourn."
> " None," said the other, " save the undone years,
> The hopelessness. Whatever hope is yours,
> Was my life also ; I went hunting wild
> After the wildest beauty in the world,
> Which lies not calm in eyes, or braided hair,
> But mocks the steady running of the hour,
> And if it grieves, grieves richlier than here.
> For by my glee might many men have laughed,
> And of my weeping something had been left,
> Which must die now. I mean the truth untold,
> The pity of war, the pity war distilled. . . .
> Courage was mine, and I had mystery,
> Wisdom was mine, and I had mastery ;
> To miss the march of this retreating world
> Into vain citadels that are not walled. . . .
> I would have poured my spirit without stint
> But not through wounds ; not on the cess of war.

Foreheads of men have bled where no wounds were.
I am the enemy you killed, my friend.
I knew you in this dark ; for so you frowned
Yesterday through me as you jabbed and killed.
I parried ; but my hands were loath and cold.
Let us sleep now. . . ."

This is interpretation and commentary at its highest. All petty and transient emotion, grief, irony, have passed away, giving place to an insight unparalleled in this kind of poetry. This absence of false emotion—irrelevant emotion—is described by Owen himself :

> The scribes on all the people shove
> And bawl allegiance to the state,
> But they who love the greater love
> Lay down their life ; they do not hate.

The unique quality of Owen's poetry is brought out clearly if we put, say, the last verse of his *Dulce et Decorum Est* beside this verse of Sassoon's :

> You smug-faced crowds with kindling eye
> Who cheer when soldier lads march by,
> Sneak home and pray you'll never know
> The hell where youth and laughter go.

Not that Sassoon has not his mood of reconciliation too. But it, too, is different from Owen's. Compare *Strange Meeting* with Sassoon's :

> Men fought like brutes ; and hideous things were done :
> And you have nourished hatred, harsh and blind.
> But in that Golgotha perhaps you'll find
> The mothers of the men who killed your son.

Owen penetrates to an even deeper meaning.

We may well ask what a poet can do in the face of such a devastating experience as modern warfare. What, at least, should he try to do ? Is it his duty to denounce war in stirring rhetoric, or to glorify his cause and his country, or to describe what he sees, or to preach a point of view ? There have been poets who have done all these things. But Wilfred Owen did very much more. He came to the war with an intense poetic sensibility, a generous and understanding nature, and an ability to penetrate to the inner reality of the experience in the midst of which he found himself. " Inner reality " is a vague term, but its definition is implied in Owen's poetry. It refers to an ability to relate these particular facts to the rest of human experience, to the life of men and women in cities and fields, to see war in its relation to all this, to appreciate just what this activity meant—what it meant as a whole and what particular aspects of it meant—in a world which was already old before the war, where happiness and suffering were no new phenomena, where men had lived diversely and foolishly and richly and gone about their occupations and were to do so again when all this was over. Owen never forgot what normal human activity was like, and always had a clear sense of its relation to the abnormal activity of war. His own table of contents gives the motive of his poem *Miners* as " How the future will forget the dead in war."

> The centuries will burn rich loads
>   With which we groaned,
> Whose warmth shall lull their dreaming lids
>   While songs are crooned.
> But they will not dream of us poor lads
>   Lost in the ground.

This is relevant comment, with no irrelevant bias. A sense of the relation of the conditions he was describing to past and future human activity is strong in Owen's poetry and helps to give it meaning and importance for the post-war generation.

Owen was no sentimentalist, but on the other hand he did not shrink from expressing the great emotional values brought out in the war. There is a world of profound feeling in his *Greater Love* :

> Red lips are not so red
>   As the stained stones kissed by the English dead.
>
> Kindness of wooed and wooer
> Seems shame to their love pure.
> O Love, your eyes lose lure
>   When I behold eyes blinded in my stead. . . .
>
> Heart, you were never hot,
>   Nor large, nor full like hearts made great with shot ;
> And though your hand be pale,
> Paler are all which trail
> Your cross through flame and hail :
>   Weep, you may weep, for you may touch them not.

" Full like hearts made great with shot "—the profound irony of the phrase is above bitterness ; and there is more than irony, there is all the suggestion of the nature of the sacrifice of youth and the pity of war without any exaggeration or hysteria. There is nothing here but the truth, the truth presented in all of its many-sided aspects simultaneously. In so much other war poetry personal irritation forces the note and twists the fact : Owen remains calm and clear-eyed and therefore all the more intense.

Even the personal note is restrained in Owen, disciplined to subjection to what must be said, what must be communicated at all costs. It is always " we " rather than " I," so that when Sassoon writes :

> . . . And you wonder why I shake you by the shoulder ;
> Drowsy, you mumble and sigh and shift your head . . .
> *You are too young to fall asleep for ever ;*
> *And when you sleep you remind me of the dead.*

Owen strikes a different note :

> —Or whether yet his thin and sodden head
> Confuses more and more with the low mould,
> His hair being one with the gray grass
> And finished fields of autumn that are old . . .
> Who knows ? Who hopes ? Who troubles ? Let it pass !
> He sleeps. He sleeps less tremulous, less cold,
> Than we who must awake, and waking, say Alas !

The difference in attitude between the two poems is fundamental. Both are effective, but while Sassoon is concerned with the pathetic as it strikes the individual, Owen's point of view is essentially *epic* in its scope and manner of treatment. It is a Homeric dirge on the dead warrior and the living

soldier. The last line might have come from the
Iliad, where we find the same almost impersonal
statement of the facts of human destiny :

"ἀλλά, φίλος, θάνε καὶ σύ· τίη ὀλοφύρεαι οὕτως;
κάτθανε καὶ Πάτροκλος, ὅ περ σέο πολλὸν ἀμείνων.
οὐχ ὁράᾳς οἷος καὶ ἐγὼ καλός τε μέγας τε;
πατρὸς δ' εἴμ' ἀγαθοῖο, θεὰ δέ με γείνατο μήτηρ·
ἀλλ' ἔπι τοι καὶ ἐμοὶ θάνατος καὶ μοῖρα κραταιή·
ἔσσεται ἢ ἠὼς ἢ δείλη ἢ μέσον ἦμαρ,
ὁππότε τις καὶ ἐμεῖο Ἄρῃ ἐκ θυμὸν ἕληται,
ἢ ὅ γε δουρὶ βαλὼν ἢ ἀπὸ νευρῆφιν ὀϊστῷ."

" Nay, friend, die thou also : wherefore dost thou lament
thus ? Even Patroclus has died, who was a better man by
far than thou. And dost thou not see what manner of man I
am, well-formed and great of stature ? My father was a
noble man, and the mother that bare me a goddess, yet
over me too hang death and mighty fate. That dawn or
eve or midday shall surely come when some one shall take
my life too in battle, whether he strike with a spear or with
an arrow from the bow." (*Iliad* xxi. 106-113.)

The tone of statement is not unlike that of
Owen.

This clarity of vision which enables him to see
and express so much at once is responsible for
some of those short verses or even phrases which
are not exhausted of meaning at the second or third
reading—passages which have an all-embracing
quality and a depth that proclaim at once the
true poet :

> For leaning out last midnight on my sill
> I heard the sighs of men . . . ,

or the concluding verse of *Training* written when
he was recovering in England in June 1918 :

> Cold winds encountered on the racing Down
> Shall thrill my heated bareness ; but awhile
> None else may meet me till I wear my Crown.

There is in Owen none of that impatience which
Sassoon often shows—impatience with those who
have been spared the consciousness of war's horrors
and its perpetual presence with them. Owen can
write, in that fine poem *The Kind Ghosts* :

> She sleeps on soft, last breaths ; but no ghost looms
> Out of the stillness of her palace wall,
> Her wall of boys on boys and dooms on dooms . . .
>
> They move not from her tapestries, their pall,
> Nor pace her terraces, their hecatombs,
> Lest aught she be disturbed, or grieved at all.

This poem is symbolic in its significance ; its
application is almost unlimited in scope. The
mood is intense, with a hint of serenity. Its
opposite is a poem like *Arms and the Boy* where the
intensity is that of a deep and sad irony. The
motive of the poem is briefly given in his table of
contents as " The unnaturalness of weapons." It
is always a simple but profound truth like this that
lies at the heart of Owen's poetry.

Owen is claimed by some modern poets as an
important influence on their poetry, but it is
difficult to see how Owen's poetry can influence
those who have so much less to say. The poet of
to-day cannot have anything as important to say

as Owen had, because his experience is more dissipated and his view of reality generally more superficial. We are not to-day brought suddenly face to face with fundamental values ; values are muddled and deceptive and our activity altogether less intense. So, although we can appreciate Owen's poetry to the full, we can learn little that will be of any help in the practice of poetry in the present age. And in fact the *content* of Owen's poetry has not influenced modern poets at all in their search for new poetic matter. The only influence at all discernible lies in the copying of that peculiar half-rhyme which Owen used so much by poets like W. H. Auden. The rhyming of " years " with " yours " and " laughed " with " left " in the passage from *Strange Meeting* quoted above is paralleled often in Auden :

> Will you turn a deaf ear
> To what they said on the shore,
> Interrogate their poises
> In their rich houses ;
>
> Of stork-legged heaven-reachers
> Of the compulsory touchers
> The sensitive amusers
> And masked amazers ? etc.

But the device is isolated and used in completely different contexts—different in manner as well as matter.

These half-rhymes of Owen are only one sign of his constant experimenting with technique and his interest in language for itself. His very earliest

I

poems show him fascinated by the manipulation of words (Mr Blunden quotes some illuminating examples of his early attempts ; the quotations he gives in his memoir are all we have), and had not the war turned his attention to other aspects of poetry there can be little doubt that he would have taken his place among those who were to help in the forging of a new poetic medium. That task is still uncompleted, a fact which gives us one more reason for wishing that Owen's career had not been cut short as it was.

What Owen's place in the development of English poetry might have been can only be a matter of conjecture, and conjecture of this kind is never very profitable. But it is enough to judge him by what he did accomplish, leaving aside all hypo-thetical questions of what he might have done. His achievement was very real. Out of his experiences in the war he fashioned poetry which expresses in rich and cogent English some of the most fundamental aspects of human thought and emotion. Amid all the horror that he encountered he preserved unscathed his sense of values and his power of intense observation and penetration, never allowing his judgment to be warped by personal bitterness or his powers of expression to be weakened through fear or prejudice. His poetry serves a double function. It stands as a lasting exposure of the pity and futility of war, and at the same time it illumines significant channels of human experience that belong to no one time and place. His poetry, he said, was not " about deeds, or lands, nor anything about glory, honour, might, majesty, dominion, or power, except War." It is because he kept those terribly clear eyes of his constantly on the object that, in writing of war, he wrote at the same time a commentary on much more than war. By limiting his aim, with an honesty of purpose rare among poets, he enlarged his achievement.

No estimate of Owen is complete without a reference to his genuine nobility of character, brought out so well in Mr Blunden's memoir with its numerous quotations from his letters. The quality is apparent, too, in his poetry—so much so, indeed, that the critic comes to a discussion of Owen's poetry with a humility not often associated with critical activity. We cannot help feeling that Owen the man was greater than the poet and that his early death involved what we may call a loss to society as great as the loss to poetry. Yet in lamenting what we lost, let us not forget what we have gained. The poetry of Wilfred Owen, slight though it is in bulk, is a rich contribution to English literature. The farther back the war years recede into the past the more clearly he stands out above the mass of war poets. Not only has his poetry an eternal plangent appeal

> To pity and whatever moans in man
> Before the last sea and the hapless stars ;
> Whatever mourns when many leave these shores ;
> Whatever shares
> The eternal reciprocity of tears,

but it remains at once a monument—small yet perfectly wrought—to the English language, and an example of how the mind of the true poet works in the face of experiences that divide him into man who suffers and artist who contemplates and understands and welds into lasting verse. He brought his suffering into his poetry sufficiently to make it genuine but not so that it warped his sense of truth. That is perhaps his greatest achievement.

February, 1936.

THE IMPORTANCE OF *ULYSSES*

WHEN a novelist wishes to build up a character in
a work of fiction he generally employs two methods.
He describes the character objectively in the most
effective prose at his command and, more important,
he endeavours to make the character reveal itself
in action. The description is generally introductory,
often intermittent, sometimes hardly present at all.
It is not absolutely necessary, and some of the
greatest writers rarely use that method—they confine
themselves to letting the character illustrate itself
in the unfolding of the story. What a man is, is
revealed by what he does. But in order that a
man may betray his character in action it is
necessary for him to be concerned in action which
is at once comprehensive in scope and representa-
tive in nature. If you ask a man the time it is
unlikely that you will learn much of his character
from his reply. You must see him in more testing
circumstances—in love, in hatred, in fear, in success,
in failure. The " plot " of a story must therefore
contain a certain number of these testing circumstances if the story is to reveal character. And, it
is generally held, if the story is also to grip the
reader the action must take the form of a story
with some degree of complication, crisis, solution.

The function of the plot is therefore twofold—to bring the characters into sufficiently testing circumstances and to keep the reader constantly interested and expectant.

James Joyce in *Ulysses* has adopted a rather different method of building up character. In the first place there is no distinction—certainly no very clear-cut distinction—between author's objective comment and description and the natural revelation of character in action. The two are rolled into one, because the comment and description are no longer external, objective, but constantly impinge on the consciousness of the character himself. Once Joyce has introduced Leopold Bloom's consciousness it remains until the end— remains even when he is not on the scene and other characters are occupying our complete attention. It is not always present in the same degree of intensity, it fades sometimes like short-wave wireless reception, but, once the first episode of the book is over, it continues to be the point of reference for almost every word in *Ulysses*. It is difficult to explain just what this means, because it is something so new both in conception and execution. Joyce does not tell a story in which Bloom figures and make Bloom act in a revealing manner, he does not bring the action to be fitted from his wardrobe of words ; he brings language to meet the action— it is the language that is fitted, moulded, controlled. Bloom is there ; he thinks, walks, talks, goes through a day's activity ; language is poured into the mould of this situation—and if language suffers a sea-change in the process it cannot be helped, the situation is more important, and eventually by its sheer reality and intensity it will *force* the words to its own significance so that by successive re-reading the situation will be made plainer and plainer as the medium becomes subdued to what employs it. It is a process that each reader has to discover for himself. Whether such a process is legitimate—whether it represents an attitude to the prose-writer's medium which can be generally useful and important—is a question we shall consider later.

There is another respect in which Joyce's method of building up a character differs from the orthodox method. He makes no attempt to present a course of action which will involve his hero in testing circumstances. There is no conventional development, crisis, resolution. We merely see Bloom throughout one day of his life—quite an ordinary day, with no startling developments, no very unusual incidents. This is not new, of course. Many writers have given contemplative portraits of a character in ordinary daily action ; but they have either depended to a great extent on objective description in order to present the character fully, or else the character is not fully described, we do not know all about him, we are not certain what he would do in *any* given circumstance. But we know absolutely everything about Bloom ; his whole nature lies completely revealed to us ; he is, in fact, one of the most rounded characters in literature. Now Joyce gives no objective description of Bloom's character, yet in this account of his hero during one day's normal activity he reveals him completely. How is it done?

It is done by several means, but largely by his brilliant use of the time dimension. He takes Bloom in one day's action—but that action includes *thought*, *retrospect* and *anticipation*. It can scarcely be doubted that any man in any day of his life has thoughts which refer back to his past and ahead to his contemplated future, but more especially to his past. Such thoughts, if given adequate expression and interpretation, will reveal the man completely with all his physical, mental, and emotional history. My reaction to everything with which I come into contact during every minute of every day is entirely conditioned by my previous history—or, if such a statement savours too much of predestination, more than 90 per cent. conditioned by my previous history. So that an adequate presentation of my reactions to, say, half-a-dozen quite ordinary phenomena will reveal, not only my character, but the historical processes by which my character comes to be what it is, to a very large degree. Joyce seems to be the first who has grasped the significance of this fact for literature. The ordinary fiction writer takes his characters through a given period of time, beginning at one point and stopping at another. Though he may glance back retrospectively at the past on occasions, or interrupt the time-sequence to tell of events which happened before the beginning of the story, in general he rigidly accepts the limitations of the moment and never thinks of exploiting the individual thought or incident in its relation to the character's consciousness in order to free himself from the tyranny of the time dimension. Consciousness, after all, is in a sense independent of time ; retrospect and anticipation are the very stuff of its being. It is the realisation of this on Joyce's part which makes him able to give such a completely rounded picture of his hero while taking him only through one day's fairly normal activities. At every point where the past impinges on the present (and how it persists in doing so in real life !) he gives it free play. Thus Bloom's character is built up gradually and completely ; the present is constantly illuminated by the past and both fuse in Bloom's consciousness. This is a point of technique in which Joyce shows himself as great an innovator as any canonised founder of a new literary school.

Not only does Joyce take every opportunity of exploiting those reactions of Bloom which are due to relevant experiences in the past ; he is also extraordinarily full and illuminating in treating of the purely contemporary aspects of Bloom's present experiences. His reactions at Dignam's funeral, on the beach with Gerty MacDowell, coming home with Stephen (to select only three out of innumerable examples), show a treatment

K

combining fullness of implication with accuracy and abundance of illuminating detail that is truly marvellous. (We may remark in passing that Joyce's detail is nearly always illuminating.)

The problem of relevant selection is one which faces every writer who tries to depict life in words. Obviously one cannot tell everything that a man says, thinks, does. If that were done (assuming that it were possible) every hour of a man's life would require a volume to itself. The writer must select, and he must select what appears to him to be most important. Now a superficial criticism of *Ulysses* might condemn it for including much irrelevant detail. But irrelevant to what? Bloom's thoughts—or, more exactly, the state of Bloom's consciousness—at the prospect of fried kidney for breakfast or on wondering how he looks to the cat are irrelevant if we wish to know what *happens* to Bloom or to be informed of those aspects of his character which make him "important" in some arbitrary sense, but on purely literary standards they are highly relevant. They help to add the third dimension to his character, to show him "in the round." Joyce is letting a character build itself with words. It is not an unlocalised character; it is in a very definite social environment (the Dublin of 1904), with very definite relations to other characters who are depicted in greater or less detail. Bloom draws himself and his environment for the contemplating reader; the picture is essentially one that rises for contemplation, and the more intensely we contemplate the clearer it appears. What is detail? We cannot say ; one aspect of Bloom is no more " detail " than another. Is a man's soul more important than his body? That is a matter of opinion. But that a man's body exists and is always making itself known and felt, that its actions and reactions are intensely important to his consciousness, is a matter of absolute fact. Thoughts are of course there as well, vague yearnings, inarticulate desires, emotions, stirrings—these go with the body and these emerge in *Ulysses* no less than the body. No less—and no more. It is not the business of the literary artist to pass judgment on a theoretical matter on which the world will always wrangle. His business is to select from life those aspects which when united will make life seem complete, or, alternatively, to present single aspects which the general experience of man agrees are significant. And what " significant " means no one can explain because we do not know enough about life and how the world works with us.

Joyce has set himself the first of these alternative aims—to select and unite aspects of experience which together will give an appearance of completeness. We can never get that sense of completeness in daily life itself, because we are always going, never arriving, always among the trees, never able to see the wood, and always *wanting* something, or *engaged* in something, never at any time able to contemplate the life we live. As long as we are alive we cannot contemplate life itself ; that will be the great function of the dead if they retain the faculties for contemplation. Those who live can only contemplate life in art, life projected on to a screen, where they themselves, striving, acting, wishing, living, are not. Joyce lets Bloom project himself on to a screen for our contemplation— Bloom and his wife and his friends and his town. That is all he does, all he wants to do. Is that a valuable activity ? Again, it is a matter of opinion. Some think that this projection of life (as distinct from the presentation of isolated aspects of it which they deem " significant ") has little value. One cannot argue about that ; one can only say (perhaps dogmatically) that the true appreciator of literary art values both activities.

Let us consider further Joyce's handling of dimensions. The orthodox writer selects and treats his material (1) in time, giving a series of events chronologically, (2) in space, dealing with events in definite localities, (3) in relevance to what *he considers* important or significant or " universal " in human life. We have seen how Joyce manages to transcend the time dimension and by careful use of psychological fact (it is to be noted that it *is* fact) fuses past, present and future into a point, as it were. As the space dimension follows and depends on time in the sense that you can only be at one place at one time this implies also to some extent an emancipation from the tyranny of place. Sometimes this emancipation is used with such licence as to be confusing. As to relevance to significant experience (and perhaps this may be considered as a dimension without bewildering the reader), Joyce here takes the line of least resistance (and most effectiveness) by surrendering his judgment to experience itself. He lets the facts decide, he lets life dictate. Having got Bloom, his wife, Dublin, and Stephen he refuses to express any judgment on values. That is not to say that there is no implicit standard of values in the book—such is implicit in the very fact that he chose Bloom, his wife, Dublin, and Stephen. He thinks that Bloom plus Dublin produce a picture of life worth contemplating, and this of course implies a standard of values as to what is worth contemplating in life. " Life itself," Joyce might answer if you asked him, but the life he presents is not quite so simple and universal as that.

But this question of values has side-tracked us. Joyce, once having made the selection, never turns back. It is Bloom's book and Dublin's book now and anything that is relevant, however remotely, at once to Bloom, to Dublin, and to this particular day in 1904 finds its way naturally into *Ulysses*. Naturally, because no allusion is forced, every throw-back into the past has its clearly seen connection with the present—with some particular event connected with Dublin, Bloom, and the day of the action. It is not a digression of the author (anything less appropriate to the technique of *Ulysses* can scarcely be imagined) nor yet a simple " Now wol

I stinte of Palamon a lyte and of Arcite forth I wol yow telle," but a deliberate and artistic exploitation of those points where the past impinges on the present in the consciousness of one of the characters.

One can understand why Joyce deliberately refrains from explaining in normal objective description the particular scene of a given part of the action. It is because nothing must come between the reader and the consciousness of the characters. That is part of Joyce's technique. He wishes the characters to take control, not in the conventional sense in which critics use that phrase, but in the sense that only what comes into the plane of consciousness of one of his characters is allowed entrance. It is not the subconscious, as some critics have maintained ; nothing is treated until it has made itself felt on the conscious level, however dimly. There is, of course, a danger in this lack of interference by the author. The reader may get bewildered, he may lose track of where he is, and so fail to make any sense out of whole scenes. This is indeed a real weakness in Joyce's method ; the activity of a man's body and mind is only comprehensible when we know their environment, and as this environment is only shown in the reactions of the characters to it, it sometimes takes a certain amount of hard brainwork on the reader's part to deduce where he is. And this is a grave defect, for that the work should be held up while the reader puzzles out where he is means serious loss in the immediacy of the effect. A very great

deal of the book is missed on the first reading and
even on the second and third ; to understand it
completely one requires a commentary such as
that provided by Mr Frank Budgen in his *James
Joyce and the Making of Ulysses.* But there can be
no doubt that what does get across comes across
magnificently. Forenoon in a newspaper office,
midday in a Dublin pub., Bloom alone with
Stephen in the early hours of the morning—these
are some of the great scenes which remain vivid
in the memory.

But Joyce is not successful in everything he tries
to do in *Ulysses.* The parallel with the *Odyssey*
remains very obscure until one has read a commentary. And what is the point of this parallel ? A
narrative which parallels the *Odyssey* at every
point is not for that reason of any value whatsoever.
Ulysses is valuable for quite other reasons, and to
learn that Stephen corresponds to Telemachus and
the opening of the second volume is an allegorical
interpretation of the Oxen of the Sun incident
may be interesting but adds nothing to our
appreciation of those scenes. Is the Gerty
MacDowell incident any truer or more effective
because it corresponds to the Nausikaa episode
in Homer ? We assume that the *Odyssey* plan
provided Joyce with a framework which he found
helpful in planning and writing his book, but the
reader finds the conception rather in the way and
certainly quite unnecessary to his appreciation of
the book.

And there are effects of style from which the reader gains nothing whatever. When Joyce chops up the newspaper-office scenes into short paragraphs with typical newspaper headlines, he goes quite as far as a writer can desirably or helpfully go in that direction. The elaborate conglomeration of styles in the beginning of the second volume, where an Anglo-Saxon heroic diction is followed successively by styles reminiscent of early English, Elizabethan, Swift, Addison, Sterne, Junius, Pater, Ruskin, and others more difficult to identify, shows quite amazing virtuosity but entirely fails to convey anything towards making the book more intelligible or effective. This symbolic use of style on Joyce's part nearly always fails signally ; it is all right in very small quantities with an easily discernible satiric effect, but used indiscriminately it is quite impossible. Not that it fails to interest or amuse ; but its place in the presentation of the story is quite obscure—in fact, Joyce fails to achieve the effect intended.

Further, this lack of complete objectivity in the use of the medium has its dangers. To put language so entirely at the service of what seeks to find expression in it, means that those stable qualities of prose which are precisely what make it a dependable medium of expression are seriously threatened. We can afford to let Joyce get away with it in *Ulysses* because the language is still stable enough to stand up to such treatment, but we simply cannot afford to allow it as a precedent. If by means of a pun, allusion, transformation, association, misunderstanding, malapropism, onomatopœia, substitution of similar sounds, and the other devices which Joyce employs more licentiously in his *Work in Progress*, language is to be transformed into something of no objectivity whatever, subject to the whims and fancies of men of unbounded verbal imagination, then it is only a question of time till no two men will write the same language. No, we cannot treat language so independently ; it is a far greater achievement to use adequately the medium that exists, to gain perfectly effective expression in words which are known and recognised than to shy at language as it is and churn unique words out of our store of associations. Joyce, let us repeat, gets away with it in *Ulysses* precisely because he is the first to do it ; if he combines portions of two words we appreciate the total effect because we know what the two original words mean and appreciate the implied confusion of ideas. But if his method be accepted as standard the stable language medium will break down and we shall have no point of reference which will give effectiveness to these creations. This, of course, applies less to *Ulysses* than to *Work in Progress*.

The importance of *Ulysses*, then, is threefold. It shows a new technique in the building up of character in fiction, it provides a brilliant method of escape from the dimensional limitations of the chronological time-sequence, and it marks the beginning of a new and dangerous treatment of

L

language as a medium. All three characteristics give the work interest ; the first two give it greatness.

For, with all its faults, *Ulysses* is a great work. It has a breadth, an almost epic quality, and at the same time a sanity and reality rare among literary productions of any generation. It is valuable for its own sake as well as important historically. It lives in the imagination of the reader as only the greatest works of art do. What reader of *Ulysses* will ever forget Leopold Bloom, that terribly complete character, or lose the vision of the paternal figure steering home the so different Stephen to Epps' Cocoa in the small hours, or cease to hear the cadences of the final paragraphs of Molly's soliloquy ? And who will forget that living Dublin through whose streets Paddy Dignam slowly rode on his last journey ? It is a book that critics may attack but which none dare call slight.

October, 1935.

THE ART OF KATHERINE MANSFIELD

I

THE short stories of Katherine Mansfield, though not many in number, contain some of the most sensitive writing in our literature. " Sensitive " is a much-abused critical term, but here it is the only one appropriate : there is in these stories a delicacy of response to life, a fine insight into the given situation, combined with a mastery of communicative phrase, that set them apart, almost as a unique species of writing. Where else can we find such a preference of reality to art together with such a perfect moulding of art to fit reality ? Katherine Mansfield's stories are not large-scale studies of the ways of man, or narratives intended to illustrate conventional values, nor are they descriptive sketches merely, studies in style, or fine treatment of language for its own sake. They are imaginative studies of situation, attempts to get " the deepest truth out of the idea," as she herself wrote in her journal. She dealt always with the single situation, the single idea, and the whole purpose of the story with its carefully chosen setting and detailed description was to bring out the meaning of this—meaning, significance, not in terms of anything external but with reference only to the truth of experience. She approached human activity from the angles provided by the isolated instance, the single combination of circumstances ; she did not approach life directly at its most exuberant, in its richest and most crowded moments, but sought to illuminate it by so presenting the aspects she selected as to bring out the " deepest truth of the idea," the reality and therefore the *relevance* of the short sequence of events she chose to isolate and present.

It is not the most obvious way of telling a story, nor is it the easiest. To make the content so dependent on the form, as it were, by relying on the method of presenting the situation in order to make it a situation worth presenting, without distorting the facts to meet the idea and without any comment, is to risk complete failure. There can be no half-success with this method ; the critic cannot say, " A thoroughly well-told story, though a little pointless," because the point is so bound up with the telling that if it cannot be brought home the telling has no purpose—indeed, no separate exist-ence—at all. This does not apply to some of the earlier stories, many of which are only descriptive sketches, or to those later stories where Katherine Mansfield deliberately takes a holiday from her normal method, but it is true of nearly all her work after *In a German Pension*. She has imposed upon herself a much severer discipline than the majority of story-tellers dare to do ; she writes only to tell the truth—not the truth for the outsider, for the observer who watches the action from the street corner, but the truth for the characters themselves and so the real meaning of the situation.

A situation can have "meaning" from many different points of view. The point of view may be ethical, or æsthetic, or dependent on any scheme of values the author wishes to apply. Katherine Mansfield consciously and deliberately avoided any such external approach. For her the meaning of the situation meant its potentialities for change in the lives of the characters, in so far as such a change had reference to aspects of experience known and appreciated by feeling and suffering beings in general. There is always this ultimate reference to life in its wider aspect, though it does not take the form of the description of the most impressive or superficially the most "significant" elements in life. It is not the course of the action itself that has this connection, but, in so many cases, this element of *change* which links up her stories with general human activity. The varying and unstable qualities of human emotions and the very essence of these qualities are illustrated by the point, the dynamic element in the story which is brought out in the presentation. It is a point the mere *observer* would miss—some subtle change of emotional atmosphere or realisation by the characters of something new, something different and cogent, though they might not themselves be aware of what it is. Thus the "truth of the idea" meant to Katherine Mansfield the meaning of the situation for those concerned in it, and this had implications far beyond the individual instance, though these implications were not stressed or commented on : this meaning she nearly always saw as involving some kind of change.

The identification of the point of a story with change can best be understood by reference to some examples. It is not, of course, an invariable feature of Katherine Mansfield's stories—some of her best are without it—but it is sufficiently predominant to be worth examining as a feature of her work. We see it in her very earliest work, *e.g.* in *The Sister of the Baroness*, the second sketch in *In a German Pension*, but here the treatment is comparatively crude and immature. The " point " of the story· is quite superficial ; it is the old theme of the lady's maid masquerading as the lady and successfully imposing on a boarding-house full of people. The change comes suddenly, at the end, as in so many of Katherine Mansfield's later stories :

" But where is my maid ? " asked the Baroness.
" There was no maid," replied the manager, " save for your gracious sister and daughter."
" Sister ! " she cried sharply. " Fool, I have no sister. My child travelled with the daughter of my dressmaker."
Tableau grandissimo !

It is an obvious and mechanical change here, with no attempt to extract " the greatest truth out of the idea " and, further, we have what in the more mature stories we never have —comment. To underline the fact as is done with the comment " Tableau grandissimo ! " gives the reader no further insight into the reality of the situation ; it merely stresses the obvious. But the story is interesting as illustrating at this early stage the beginnings of what was to be one of the most important features of Katherine Mansfield's technique.

Later examples of this " peripeteia " are abundant. In *The Garden Party* the story rests on the change from the party atmosphere to the atmosphere of sudden death in the carter's cottage, and the *meaning* of that change. All the other elements, the description, the dialogue, the character sketching, are subordinated to this. In *Her First Ball* the point of the story lies in the change of mood :

> Leila gave a light little laugh, but she did not feel like laughing. Was it—could it all be true ? It sounded terribly true. Was this first ball only the beginning of her last ball after all ? At that the music seemed to change ; it sounded sad, sad ; it rose upon a great sigh. Oh, how quickly things changed ! Why didn't happiness last for ever ? For ever wasn't a bit too long.

And the story concludes with a change back to the original mood.

The Singing Lesson is perhaps the most obvious example of all—a little too obvious to be really effective. The story describes first the mood of a singing teacher giving her lesson in school after receiving a letter that morning from her fiancé breaking off the engagement, and concludes with her sudden change of mood after receiving a telegram telling her to pay no regard to the letter. Here the change comes right at the end, and that

is its usual place in the stories. *The Stranger* describes
an impatient husband waiting for the entrance into
harbour of the liner which brings back to him his
wife after she has been away for ten months. His
longing to possess her again and his anticipation
of a blissful reunion is perfectly conveyed—and
then comes the change when, once they are in the
hotel together, she tells him how one of the passengers
had died on board the previous night :

> " Oh, it wasn't anything in the least infectious ! " said
> Janey. She was speaking scarcely above her breath. " It was
> *heart*." A pause. " Poor fellow ! " she said. " Quite young."
> And she watched the fire flicker and fall. " He died in my
> arms," said Janey.

And the story ends :

> " You're not—sorry I told you, John, darling ? It hasn't
> made you sad ? It hasn't spoilt our evening—our being alone
> together ? "
> But at that he had to hide his face. He put his face into
> her bosom and his arms enfolded her.
> Spoilt their evening ! Spoilt their being alone together !
> They would never be alone together again.

This stress on the significance of change comes in
again and again. *Revelations* depends on the change
wrought in Monica's mood by the death of her
hairdresser's little girl. In *Bliss* the change comes
at the very end, when Bertha's mood of glorious
well-being, which has been the theme of the story
up to the last page, collapses like a burst balloon
as a result of what she sees in the hall when her
husband is showing out the guests. Even in her

unfinished stories we see the stage set for the peripeteia. In *The Doves' Nest* everything is there but the final change to give point to the story, and this is true also of *Father and the Girls*, *Honesty*, and *Second Violin*. In *Widowed* and *Susannah* the change has already come.

The uniqueness of Katherine Mansfield's method of giving point to what has gone before by the sudden twist at the end can be best appreciated by comparing her technique with that of some other short-story writers. A really illuminating comparison is that of James Joyce's story *The Dead* (the last in *Dubliners*) and Katherine Mansfield's *The Stranger*, the conclusion of which has already been quoted. Both have similar themes—the change produced in a man who is longing passionately to be alone with his wife on learning that her mood is the result of something quite unconnected with himself, something that has reference to an experience he does not share and which he feels is coming between them and their love. In Joyce the development of the story is much slower, much more deliberate, and the final point emerges gradually in the course of the narrative. Gabriel and Gretta are at a party, the annual dance given by the Misses Morkan, Gabriel's aunts. The description of the party occupies about forty pages ; it is detailed and convincing. Just when most of the guests are leaving, and Gabriel is standing in the hall waiting for his wife, they hear some one singing upstairs :

M

The song seemed to be in the old Irish tonality and the singer seemed uncertain both of his words and of his voice. The voice, made plaintive by distance and by the singer's hoarseness, faintly illuminated the cadence of the air with words expressing grief. . . .

"O," exclaimed Mary Jane. "It's Bartell D'Arcy singing, and he wouldn't sing all the night. O, I'll get him to sing a song before he goes."

"O, do, Mary Jane," said Aunt Kate.

Mary Jane brushed past the others and ran to the staircase, but before she reached it the singing stopped and the piano was closed abruptly.

"O, what a pity!" she cried. "Is he coming down, Gretta?"

Gabriel heard his wife answer yes and saw her come down towards them. . . .

There is no immediate further reference to the song. A description of the walk home follows. Gabriel is walking behind his wife:

She was walking on before him so lightly and so erect that he longed to run after her noiselessly, catch her by the shoulders and say something foolish and affectionate into her ear. She seemed to him so frail that he longed to defend her against something and then to be alone with her. Moments of their secret life together burst like stars upon his memory.

. . . He longed to be alone with her. When the others had gone away, when he and she were alone in the room in the hotel, then they would be alone together. He would call her softly:

"Gretta!"

Perhaps she would not hear at once: she would be undressing. Then something in his voice would strike her. She would turn and look at him. . . .

But once they are alone together it comes out that that song had reminded Gretta of a young

boy who had been in love with her, who had died
as a result of pneumonia developed after standing
in her garden in the rain when he came to pay his
last visit to her. Unlike Katherine Mansfield,
Joyce does not conclude the story immediately with
an indication of Gabriel's change of mood on
learning this. Gabriel lies in bed awake and thinks
it over ; he sinks into a reverie where the truth of
the situation is revealed to him and all bitterness
departs from him as he thinks of the dead boy,
gradually losing his own identity in the reverie.
As he falls asleep snow begins to fall outside :

He watched sleepily the flakes, silver and dark, falling
obliquely against the lamplight. The time had come for him
to set out on his journey westward. Yes, the newspapers were
right : snow was general all over Ireland. It was falling on
every part of the dark central plain, on the treeless hills,
falling softly upon the bog of Allen and, farther westward,
softly falling into the dark mutinous Shannon waves. It was
falling, too, upon every part of the lonely churchyard on the
hill where Michael Furey lay buried. It lay thickly drifted
on the crooked crosses and headstones, on the spears of the
little gate, on the barren thorns. His soul swooned slowly
as he heard the snow falling faintly through the universe and
faintly falling, like the descent of their last end, upon all the
living and the dead.

This is one way of getting " the deepest truth
out of the idea "—to put extended comment of this
kind into the mind of the character affected so
that everything relevant is said, the meaning stated,
the point brought out. But with Katherine
Mansfield much more depends on the actual

presentation of the story. Neither she nor her characters make lengthy comment ; the meaning of the situation is never *stated*, but implied. Her endeavour is to put the story in a position to illuminate itself ; the parts throw light on the whole and the whole throws light on the parts so that, for example, the change at the end puts new meaning into what has gone before, putting everything into a new perspective which we had not been aware of until we arrived at the end. Joyce's method is more discursive, less economical, though quite as effective in its own way. But this difference in technique must not blind us to the many points of similarity between Joyce's *Dubliners* and Katherine Mansfield's stories. *Ivy Day in the Committee Room*, though so different in theme, is similar in " texture " to that little masterpiece *The Daughters of the Late Colonel*, one of the more static of Katherine Mansfield's stories. Both have that quiet observation and penetrating selection of detail so effective in creating atmosphere. Joyce's story, *A Painful Case*, shows at once the points of resemblance and the points of difference between the two writers. Comparison of this kind could be prolonged indefinitely.

Katherine Mansfield seems to have been always on her guard against any lapses from the ideal of strict self-restraint which she imposed upon herself in dealing with emotional crises. Mr Middleton Murry tells us in his introductory note to *Something Childish and Other Stories* that " *Sixpence* was excluded from ' The Garden Party and Other Stories ' by Katherine Mansfield because she thought it ' sentimental.' " And after describing an imaginary scene—*The New Baby*—in her journal, she adds :

You ought to keep this, my girl, just as a *warning* to show what an arch-wallower you *can* be.

That she had a tendency in this direction is shown by occasional false touches throughout her work. *Miss Brill*, for example, the pathetic story of the governess out for her weekly walk in the park wearing, after a long interval, her beloved fur, which is audibly described by a giggling girl as looking " exactly like a fried whiting," concludes thus :

But to-day she passed the baker's by, climbed the stairs, went into the little dark room—her room like a cupboard— and sat down on the red eiderdown. She sat there for a long time. The box that the fur came out of was on the bed. She unclasped the necklet quickly ; quickly, without looking, laid it aside. But when she put the lid on she thought she heard something crying.

Here the emotion seems to be stressed in the wrong place. The " truth of the idea " lies in the change of mood when Miss Brill, in the midst of her exultation, the feeling that she is an actor among fellow-actors in this bright morning scene, suddenly learns the truth from the chance remark of a girl. As a rule Katherine Mansfield manages to bring out the significance of a situation with greater economy and a surer touch. In *The Man without a Temperament* there is the same suggestion of sentimentality in the ending, but here it is adequately balanced by the facts, as it were ; the contrast between the Englishman abroad as he appears to the foreign observers and the Englishman alone with his wife is the whole point of the story ; it is a case where the truth itself is sentimental :

. . . He went over to the washstand and dipt his fingers in water. " Are you all right now ? Shall I switch off the light ? "

" Yes, please. No. Boogles ! Come back here a moment. Sit down by me. Give me your hand." She turns his signet-ring. " Why weren't you asleep ? Boogles, listen. Come closer. I sometimes wonder—do you mind awfully being out here with me ? "

He bends down. He kisses her. He tucks her in, he smoothes the pillow.

" Rot ! " he whispers.

Sentimental, perhaps, but there is no other way of doing it—except to tell a different story.

Objective truth was always Katherine Mansfield's aim in her stories. She wished to become the supreme recorder, free from all personal bias and even interest. " I can't tell the truth about Aunt Anne unless I am free to enter into her life without self-consciousness," she wrote in her journal in 1921. She was reproaching herself for not being calm enough when writing. " Calm yourself. Clear yourself. And anything that I write in this mood will be no good ; it will be full of *sediment*. . . . One must learn, one must practise to *forget* oneself." Yet sometimes the reader is left a little in doubt whether the story is told in terms of the thought

of the observer or the observed. The meaning of
the situation is the meaning for those concerned
in it, but occasionally we find the writer herself
entering into the situation for an instant. In the
beginning of *The Doll's House* she is describing the
emotions of the children on receiving the present
of a doll's house :

> The hook at the side was stuck fast. Pat prized it open
> with his penknife, and the whole house front swung back,
> and—there you were, gazing at one and the same moment
> into the drawing-room and dining-room, the kitchen and
> two bedrooms. That is the way for a house to open ! Why
> don't all houses open like that ? How much more exciting
> than peering through the slit of a door into a mean little hall
> with a hatstand and two umbrellas ! That is—isn't it ?—
> what you long to know about a house when you put your
> hand on the knocker. Perhaps it is the way God opens houses
> at the dead of night when He is taking a quiet turn with an
> angel. . . .

In the last two sentences of this paragraph
Katherine Mansfield has substituted her own mind
for that of the children. The thought at the end
is not a child's thought; it is her own. From
describing the working of a child's imagination she
has slipped almost imperceptibly into giving an
example of the working of her own. We find this
occasionally throughout the stories—the spectator
becoming too interested to hold aloof and allowing
her own consciousness to enter. It is just because
her approach is usually so objective that we notice
those occasions where, only for a moment, she
allows the subjective element to enter. Of course,

in pure description the author must talk to some extent in her own person, but once the characters are set going and the story is told in terms of *their* minds any intrusion by the author is dangerous. There are few authors who intrude so rarely as Katherine Mansfield, who, when she does intrude, does it in this almost imperceptible way, substituting her own imagination directly just for a sentence or two ; and perhaps to note those occasions when she lapses from her own rule is cavilling criticism. Certainly it needs an eagle eye to spot the examples, and *The Doll's House* remains one of her most perfect stories in spite of this brief intrusion. But we can imagine how effective a *child's* simile might have been in that passage, especially one created by Katherine Mansfield, one of whose greatest qualities is her insight into the child mind.

It is always difficult, in describing the significance of a situation for those concerned in it, to avoid letting one's own sense of significance intrude unconsciously. It requires such a high degree of imagination to tell the truth. Only in her less successful moments does Katherine Mansfield give us some notion of the difficulty of the achievement involved in her successful work. Her writing at its best has a purity rare in literature. She never attempted to put into a story more than " the truth of the idea " warranted. " The truth is one can get only *so much* into a story ; there is always a sacrifice," she wrote in her journal. It was a sacrifice she was constantly making. She always

kept her eye strictly on the object, trying to probe
to its inner meaning and reality by sheer intensity
of observation. She wrote no more than she saw,
but she saw so much in the least human activity
that she never needed to do more than record her
observations. In the best of her work—in *At the
Bay, The Doll's House, Prelude, The Daughters of the
Late Colonel*—art and life are identified to a unique
degree for the very reason that art as such is never
allowed to obtrude.

II

There is more in Katherine Mansfield's stories
than the " point," the extracting of " the truth of
the idea." The moment of insight is always
prepared for, the setting of the story is always
adequate and convincing ; the descriptive passages
are often brilliantly done. A consideration of her
technique in description will reveal some of her
finest qualities as a writer. It is, after all, the
description, the creation of atmosphere, that makes
At the Bay, The Garden Party and *Prelude* so memor-
able. One of the reasons for her success here is
that the scenes described were real scenes,
remembered with great vividness from her own
early experience. Those aspects of New Zealand
landscape especially, which occur so frequently
in her work, are presented with a concreteness and
a reality which are largely responsible for that
quality of freshness that pervades her writing. The
first section of *At the Bay* provides one of the finest

N

examples of her descriptive technique. It starts
quite simply with a statement of the time : " Very
early morning." Then immediately the phrase is
localised : " The sun was not yet risen, and the
whole of Crescent Bay was hidden under a white
sea-mist." There follows a selection of details, not
sufficient to be tedious, just enough to give the
reader an adequate visual picture and a sense of
atmosphere. First the hills behind, covered with
mist, and a suggestion of what the mist concealed ;
then a description of the big drops of dew hanging
on the bushes. The first paragraph ends with a
characteristic imaginative touch :

> It looked as though the sea had beaten up softly in the
> darkness, as though one immense wave had come rippling,
> rippling—how far ? Perhaps if you had waked up in the
> middle of the night you might have seen a big fish flicking
> in at the window and gone again. . . .

The descriptive details are informed with life by
this impinging of the human mind on their objective
passivity. And it is no fault here that Katherine
Mansfield looked at the scene in terms of her *own*
imagination, because she has not yet introduced
the characters who are to take control. We see in
this first paragraph the creation of atmosphere by
the selection and arrangement of detail lit up by a
touch of human imagination. Thus the emotional
potentialities of the landscape are indicated. It is
not enough for the story-teller to describe a scene
for its own sake, leaving it as a passive background
for the action. Some relation must be established

between the setting and the action, human values must pervade *everything* in a story if it is to be really organic in structure. That is why the description in Hardy's novels is so much more integral to the story than that in Scott. Scott's description often takes the form of preliminary set pieces, which, however effective in themselves, are not sufficiently related to the human significance of the story to be really one with it. With Katherine Mansfield, as, in so different ways, with Hardy and Conrad, there is no such isolation of the descriptive element.

But to return to the opening of *At the Bay*. After the first paragraph, with its selection of detail and enlivening imaginative element, there is a quick return to the sea, this time its audible (not its visual) qualities being noted :

> Ah-Aah! sounded the sleepy sea. And from the bush there came the sound of little streams flowing, quickly, lightly, slipping between the smooth stones, gushing into ferny basins and out again ; and there was the splashing of big drops on large leaves, and something else—what was it?—a faint stirring and shaking, the snapping of a twig and then such silence that it seemed some one was listening.

One could write a whole essay on style from a consideration of the effect of the juxtaposition of this paragraph and the previous. We see how the scene is built up while at the same time the reader is gradually enwrapped in the appropriate atmosphere. Early morning—white mist—bungalows— heavy dew—mist merging beach and sea—sea rippling up in the darkness. *Then* our escape is finally cut off by our hearing the moaning of the sleepy sea in the background. We are caught in the atmosphere now ; it is all round us. That little sentence, " Ah-Aah ! sounded the sleepy sea," gains supreme effect by being in just the right place. It comes after a pause, after the misty bay has been presented to our sight and to our imagination. It is as though we were bidden to stand quite still and hear what had been going on all the time without our realising. Everything has become quite quiet and we can hear the sea. And, our ears now becoming sensitive to what is going on, the next moment we hear too the sound of the little streams and the splashing of big drops on large leaves. It is not only the selection of right detail that matters, but the *order* in which it is presented to the reader.

We see exactly the same technique in the opening of section 5 of *Prelude* :

Dawn came sharp and chill with red clouds on a faint green sky and drops of water on every leaf and blade. A breeze blew over the garden, dropping dew and dropping petals, shivered over the drenched paddocks, and was lost in the sombre bush. In the sky some tiny stars floated for a moment and then they were gone—they were dissolved like bubbles. And plain to be heard in the early quiet was the sound of the creek in the paddock running over the brown stones, running in and out of the sandy hollows, hiding under clumps of dark berry bushes, spilling into a swarm of yellow water flowers and cresses.

Here again the reality of the scene is finally emphasised by the sound of water.

The opening section of *At the Bay* concludes with a detailed description of a shepherd going up the road with his flock of sheep. It is the final touch to the setting before the curtain rises, and provides also a way of incidentally describing the disappearance of the mist and the alteration in the appearance of the landscape as the morning advances.

The sun was rising. It was marvellous how quickly the mist thinned, sped away, dissolved from the shallow plain, rolled up from the bush and was gone as if in a hurry to escape ; big twists and curls jostled and shouldered each other as the silvery beams broadened. The far-away sky— a bright, pure blue—was reflected in the puddles, and the drops, swimming along the telegraph poles, flashed into points of light. Now the leaping, glittering sea was so bright it made one's eyes ache to look at it. [Perhaps this last phrase represents the intrusion of a foreign personal element ; there was no one to see the sea except the shepherd, and his eyes were not aching—or if they were, we should have been told that his eyes were meant. It is arguable whether " one's eyes " is not a false touch.] The shepherd drew a pipe, the bowl as small as an acorn, out of his breast pocket, fumbled for a chunk of speckled tobacco, pared off a few shavings and stuffed the bowl. He was a grave, fine-looking old man. As he lit up and the blue smoke wreathed his head, the dog, watching, looked proud of him.

Then the sheep go past the bungalows, an opportunity to describe what is happening there, with just a hint of the drowsy heads inside and a description of Florrie, the Burnells' cat, sitting on the gate-post waiting for the milk-girl. The opening section concludes with the disappearance of the sheep. All is quiet again, and the stage is set for the appearance of the principal characters :

The shepherd put away his pipe, dropping it into his breast-pocket so that the bowl hung over. And straightway the soft airy whistling began again. Wag ran out along a ledge of rock after something that smelled, and ran back again disgusted. Then pushing, nudging, hurrying, the sheep rounded the bend and the shepherd followed after out of sight.

The cadence of that last sentence is at once a fitting close to the introductory scene and a preparation for what is to follow.

It would be pleasant and interesting to follow *At the Bay* section by section to its close, noting at every point those aspects of Katherine Mansfield's descriptive technique which contribute to the success of the story. But we have space to mention only the more characteristic touches. Notice the introduction of Kezia :

" Oh, Kezia ! Why are you such a messy child ! " cried Beryl despairingly.

" Me, Aunt Beryl ? " Kezia stared at her. What had she done now ? She had only dug a river down the middle of her porridge, filled it, and was eating the banks away. But she did that every single morning, and no one had said a word up till now.

" Why can't you eat your food properly like Isabel and Lottie ? " How unfair grownups are !

" But Lottie always makes a floating island, don't you, Lottie ? "

" I don't," said Isabel smartly. " I just sprinkle mine with sugar and put on the milk and finish it. Only babies play with their food."

Right at the beginning the children are revealed as real children, without any formal description or psychologising. Not only that, but the very first things they say differentiate them one from another and reveal their relative ages and positions in the family. Katherine Mansfield always shows a remarkable understanding of children, and the Burnell children are some of the most convincing in literature.

The handling of Stanley is equally competent, though perhaps not quite so all-embracing in scope. Again and again in Katherine Mansfield's work we find reflected an impatience with the man about the house, with stress on his helplessness, fussiness, and unconscious selfishness.

Oh, the relief, the difference it made to have the man out of the house. Their very voices were changed as they called to one another ; they sounded warm and loving and as if they shared a secret. Beryl went over to the table. " Have another cup of tea, mother. It's still hot." She wanted, somehow, to celebrate the fact that they could do what they liked now. There was no man to disturb them ; the whole perfect day was theirs.

The scene on the beach is the liveliest of all. There is here a penetrating observation of relevant detail that gives an extraordinary vital quality to the writing. Here, too, the order in which the details are presented is always the most effective, producing subtler elements of surprise and contrast. That every phrase was carefully chosen for its appropriateness in its context is shown by the fact that some are taken from passages written earlier in the journal, deliberately polished up and put in

their new setting. For example, this is from
Morning Children, written in the journal in 1920 :

> . . . And now there is the sound of plunging water, and all
> those youthful, warm bodies, the tender exposed boy children,
> and the firm compact little girls, lie down in the bath tubs
> and ruffle their shoulders scattering the bright drops as birds
> love to do with their wings.

And this is from *At the Bay*, where the children
are described going into the water :

> The firm compact little girls were not half so brave as the
> tender, delicate-looking little boys. . . .

There are many examples of re-writing of passages
that had been written earlier as jottings in the
journal.

The Daughters of the Late Colonel shows Katherine
Mansfield in another mood, but is equally typical
of her method of creating atmosphere. Unlike
most of her stories, it contains no sudden change
at the end ; it is more even in tone and the same
mood remains all through. Here again the main
feature is the quiet arrangement of detail, and
purely by means of effective arrangement every
ounce of meaning is squeezed out of slight and
casual incidents. Nothing is superfluous, nothing
is mere decoration or trimming, everything has
its part to play in producing the required effect.

> But the strain told on them when they were back in the
> dining-room. They sat down, very shaky, and looked at
> each other.
> " I don't feel I can settle to anything," said Josephine,

" until I've had something. Do you think we could ask Kate
for two cups of hot water ? "
" I really don't see why we shouldn't," said Constantia
carefully. She was quite normal again. " I won't ring. I'll
go to the kitchen door and ask her."
" Yes, do," said Josephine, sinking down into a chair.
" Tell her, just two cups, Con, nothing else—on a tray." . . .
Their cold lips quivered at the greenish brims. Josephine
curved her small red hands round the cup ; Constantia sat
up and blew on the wavy steam, making it flutter from one
side to the other.

Every detail here is relevant. The cups of hot
water, Josephine curving her small red hands
round the cup, the attitude to Kate ("just two
cups, Con, nothing else " and " I'll go to the kitchen
door and ask her "), Constantia blowing the steam
—all this shows that quiet and pertinent observation utilised to create atmosphere. Everything has
reference to the *mood* of the story, everything is
organised so as to bring " the deepest truth out of
the idea." It is largely a matter of selection and
method of presentation. That so much should be
achieved by such an economy of means is the
greatest tribute to Katherine Mansfield's technique.
The Daughters of the Late Colonel is a landmark in
the history of the English short story.

To record objectively, with nevertheless complete
understanding and complete knowledge of every
aspect of the situation, was Katherine Mansfield's
aim. This reconciling of complete objectivity with
complete knowledge implies a constant state of
unstable equilibrium on the part of the author.

She could not impose her own consciousness too much on the situation, yet at the same time she had to employ her own imagination and sensibility in recording it. The older writers solved the problem by leaving themselves free to observe and comment in their own person. From Fielding through Thackeray right on to the present day this practice has continued, different authors making use of it in differing degrees. Joyce, in *Ulysses*, solves the problem in a completely different way : he presents everything through the consciousness of his characters, never appearing in his own person at all, never even *observing* in his own person.[1] Nothing is known absolutely, only in so far as it impinges on the consciousness of one or other of his characters. Katherine Mansfield's method lies somewhere between the traditional one and that of Joyce and other modern writers. She refuses to sacrifice her powers of independent observation, but at the same time she takes note of nothing which is not in the highest sense relevant to the situation she is presenting. She frees herself by a deliberate effort from any irrelevant emotion or pre-supposition. " One must learn, one must practise to *forget* oneself. I can't tell the truth about Aunt Anne until I am free to enter into her life without self-consciousness." To enter Aunt Anne's life—yes, but retaining her own powers of insight and imagination, her own interest in human

[1] This, too, is the method of the " epistolary " novel, as used *e.g.* by Richardson, but the technique here is clumsier.

emotion, her own curiosity and truthfulness. " Lord, make me crystal clear for thy light to shine through," she wrote in her journal, but the process could not be as simple as that—it might be compared rather to refraction.

This ability to put her own mind inside other people's sometimes led Katherine Mansfield to substitute her own sensitive reactions for those appropriate to the character. The unstable equilibrium could not be maintained over a long period without occasional wavering. We have seen how, in entering into the mind of a child, she lets herself on one occasion introduce a piece of imagination quite unchildlike in quality. It is a slight point, but interesting as indicative of the difficulty of her method. Now and again we find her more articulate about the emotions of her characters, more conscious of their real nature, than the characters themselves could be. The nameless heroine of *Psychology* lets her visitor go without having established the contact with him she intended :

She was right. He did see nothing at all. Misery ! He'd missed it. It was too late to do anything now. Was it too late ? Yes, it was. A cold snatch of hateful wind blew into the garden. Curse life ! He heard her cry " au revoir " and the door slammed.

There is no fault to find here. A mood of which the character was quite conscious has been adequately rendered into words. It does not matter if the character herself would not have used those actual words : they represent what she might have thought, her mood being potentially quite articulate. But the story continues :

> Running back into the studio she behaved so strangely. She ran up and down lifting her arms and crying : " Oh ! Oh ! How stupid ! How imbecile ! How stupid ! " And then she flung herself down on the *sommier* thinking of nothing —just lying there in her rage. All was over. What was over ? Oh—something was . . .

But would the character herself have been conscious of these things ? Has not Katherine Mansfield here substituted her own sensitive and interested mind so that the character is portrayed as being articulate about what she could not consciously have had any knowledge of ? " And then she flung herself down on the *sommier* thinking of nothing—just lying there in her rage." That is convincing, and seems to convey the truth of the situation. But to put into the mind of a girl who was enraged without knowing why, who is lying thinking of nothing, the conscious thought that " all was over. What was over ? Oh—something was " — this is to allow the author's objective comment to masquerade as part of the consciousness of the character. Sometimes Katherine Mansfield succumbs to the temptation of substituting her own clear vision for the blindness of those whose reactions she is portraying. But she never does this sufficiently to interfere with the reality of the story or with that creation of atmosphere which is one of her greatest achievements.

III

It is interesting to trace the development of Katherine Mansfield's art from the comparatively immature *In a German Pension* to her last stories. Her earliest work is little more than journalism, though journalism of the very finest kind. We see her exercising her powers of observation and expression, taking in everything that goes on around her, noting scenes and incidents because they amused or angered her. There is no organising of detail in the service of " the deepest truth of the idea." There is, too, a vein of irony in this early work which later gives way to something more profound. The opening paragraph of *Frau Fischer* is typical of her style and attitude at this stage :

Frau Fischer was the fortunate possessor of a candle factory somewhere on the banks of the Eger, and once a year she ceased from her labours to make a " cure " in Dorschausen, arriving with a dress-basket neatly covered in a black tarpaulin and a hand-bag. The latter contained amongst her handkerchiefs, eau de Cologne, toothpicks, and a certain woollen muffler very comforting to the " magen," samples of her skill in candle-making, to be offered up as tokens of thanksgiving when her holiday time was over.

There is a sense of " clever writing " here which we do not find in the later work. And when she does introduce a " point " into these early sketches it is often almost melodramatic in effect, as in *The Child-Who-Was-Tired* (with its crude Tchekov influence) and *The Swing of the Pendulum*. There is little of that quietness of tone which is so important in her best stories. *A Birthday* is the only story in *In a German Pension* which shows something of that calm intensity one associates with Katherine Mansfield's writing. The others in this collection are either mere descriptive sketches with an ironical flavour, or else rather stark attempts at naturalism. But already we see that observation which was to serve her in such good stead later, though without the organising power and brilliant technique that came with practice and experience.

Something Childish is a collection which contains more of Katherine Mansfield's earlier work, and some of the stories here are very interesting for their anticipation of later themes. The " Cinderella reverie " theme occurs in *The Tiredness of Rosabel*— written as early as 1908, Mr Middleton Murry tells us, when Katherine Mansfield was only nineteen— which can be compared with the many later handlings of the same subject. The meditations of Beryl, in the Burnell stories, have a similar flavour, though the setting is entirely different. A comparison of the ending of *The Tiredness of Rosabel* with that of *At the Bay* (whose last section has some similarity to the latter half of the earlier story) is instructive. *At the Bay* concludes thus :

A cloud, small, serene, floated across the moon. In that moment of darkness the sea sounded deep, troubled. Then the cloud sailed away, and the sound of the sea was a vague murmur, as though it waked out of a dark dream. All was still.

And this is the concluding paragraph of *The Tiredness of Rosabel* :

And the night passed. Presently the cold fingers of dawn closed over her uncovered hand ; grey light flooded the dull room. Rosabel shivered, drew a little gasping breath, sat up. And because her heritage was that tragic optimism, which is all too often the only inheritance of youth, still half asleep, she smiled, with a little nervous tremor round her mouth.

In the early passage Katherine Mansfield goes back to comment on the situation, to relate her description of the dawn to her description of the heroine. Her later method is subtler. There is no comment, there is no reversion to the principal character, only the quiet statement of fact which produces its own effect. The difference between these two passages is typical of one aspect of the difference between her earlier and her later work. In Katherine Mansfield's development as a writer we see an increasing economy of means, until in her most mature work, including those unfinished stories collected in *The Doves' Nest*, there is not a word which does not contribute to the illumination of the situation ; her control over language is complete, reaching a degree that few other writers have attained.

Power of observation Katherine Mansfield had from the beginning ; it is the use she makes of this power that develops as her art matures. The mastery of arrangement shown in *At the Bay*, where silence, broken only by the sound of the sea, is the permanent background of the story, coming to the foreground only in between the scenes and at the beginning and end, is one of the finest examples of her technique in maturity. The marshalling of detail in *The Daughters of the Late Colonel* has already been noted ; it shows a sense of the organic nature of the relation of the parts of a story to the whole which is absent in her earliest work and indeed in the great majority of all literary work produced in English. English literature in general is characterised by a love for the loosely knit and a lack of sense of form which are not faults of Katherine Mansfield.

The descriptive sketches based on her experiences in France during the war years occupy a middle place in Katherine Mansfield's development. *An Indiscreet Journey* may be compared with passages written in her journal about the same time. It is primarily a description of some of her own experiences, but reference to the corresponding passages in the journal show that she has made a deliberate attempt to *organise* the details so as to extract a maximum of meaning from the situation. She is gradually approaching the realisation that the aim of her kind of writing is to " get the deepest truth out of the idea." It is as late as July 1921 that we meet this phrase in her journal. She was engaged then in writing the last of the stories that appear in *The Garden Party* (as we learn from Mr Middleton Murry's introductory note to that volume) and was just about to write *At the Bay*.

We can see the influence that the formulation of this aim had on her work.

Katherine Mansfield's development was the result of increased consciousness of what she wanted to achieve in her writing. She was not one of those writers who improve with practice automatically. She saw quite clearly the gap between her achievement and her aim—a bigger gap to her sight than it is to ours—and set herself to remove it. To read her journal alongside her stories is to realise how deliberately she disciplined herself in response to the high ideal that was always before her. It was not that she wanted her work to be impressive or important ; she wanted only that it should correspond to her sense of truth. She had not to search for her themes ; that power of observation and insight that was always with her provided her with more material than she was able to use. "There is so much to do, and I do so little," she wrote in her journal. "Look at the stories that wait and wait just at the threshold." She felt that life awaited her pen, and that her duty was to embody it *truly* in her art. And always it was through the single situation that she approached truth of reality.

The time has come when we can look back on Katherine Mansfield's work and place it in its true perspective. We can see it now as one of the greatest contributions to the development of the art of the short story ever made. Her work has shown new possibilities for the small-scale writer, and by the uniqueness of its achievement points the way to a new critical approach to that age-long problem, the relation of " art " to " life." No writer in either the creative or the critical field has yet shown himself of the calibre to profit to the full from this twofold contribution to literature.

March, 1936.

THE JUDGING OF CONTEMPORARY LITERATURE

PERHAPS criticism has always appeared to be in a chaotic state to the contemporary observer. Certainly to-day it seems to be in a state of unprecedented confusion. Among the more serious critics there is no agreement at all concerning the nature of literary value, while most critics of the periodical press agree at least in superficiality and ineffectiveness. It is not so much that we lack standards by which to judge as that we differ hopelessly on what it is we are judging. One critic praises a novel because it is written in a flowing English ; another condemns it because it portrays a kind of life that can only be found in occasional corners of the worst city slums ; a third praises it because it establishes contact with the proletariat ; another condemns it because it belongs to no tradition of writing ; yet a fifth praises it for the same reason ; a further critic praises it for the insight and detailed observation shown in the description of a lamp-post at midnight. The catalogue might be extended indefinitely. Differences of opinion are natural and to a certain extent desirable, but differences of this kind—differences which show the critics quite unconcerned to isolate those factors in a work of literature which determine its value as literature—indicate a very disturbing state of affairs.

We need to-day a keener sense of literary value. This is not to say that we require a set of rules whose application will reveal the worth of a book. It is a sense of the uniqueness of literary value that is required—its difference from, at least its relation to, other values. We can allow differences concerning the nature of this value, but we must demand agreement on its existence if criticism is to serve any literary function at all. Criticism at present is serving several functions—psychological, sociological, political, ethical, even metaphysical— and in so far as it serves these functions adequately it is valuable, but when criticism fulfilling any or all of these functions masquerades indiscriminately as "literary" the resulting confusion is overwhelming. The sociologist will find a value in Dickens, the psychologist a value in Shakespeare, the feminist a value in Meredith, and other specialists will find other values in the same writers. But literary worth is distinct—even if, as some hold, it is composite— and to allow this fact to be obscured is ultimately to oust literature from the world of art altogether and to deny any usefulness to writing which cannot be viewed as the handmaid of some scientific or epistemological activity. That the present tendency in criticism is already helping to produce an inferiority complex among imaginative writers and academic critics—especially the latter—can be judged from the increasing habit of stressing the

" difficulty " of literature (it requires as painstaking work as science, in fact) and dwelling on the laboratory methods of *e.g.* Shakespearean criticism as a means of justification.

It may be argued that to seek for a purely literary value is to divorce literature from life, but that is to miss the point : literature has its own relation to life—closer than that of psychology or philosophy—and it is precisely in order that this relation should not be obscured that its uniqueness should be understood and appreciated. It is doing no service to literature to identify the value of poetry with its value for the psychologist or the worth of fiction with its interest to the sociologist. That may be one way of increasing the reading public, but it requires little argument to prove that sooner or later the reaction on literature is going to be most harmful.

Perhaps this confusion of values is partly self-induced by the critics as a means of escape from the uncomfortable problem of how to judge contemporary literature. The worst work is always *interesting* from one point of view or another—indeed the worse the work often the more interesting it is. To the psycho-analyst, bad poetry is as helpful as good in investigating the mental processes at work : in the unfinished second-rate product the processes may stand more clearly revealed. So the modern critic can always justify his errors of judgment by appealing to some particular specialist and explaining that it was to *him* the work was interesting and that's what he meant all along. But we cannot allow such specious methods, and the problem of judging our contemporaries must be faced squarely.

And it is a problem. Let anyone who doubts it study the early nineteenth century reviews and make a list of the appalling errors of judgment committed by some really fine minds. Let them consider what some intelligent contemporaries thought of Wordsworth and Coleridge and Keats— political prejudice apart—and remember Scott's opinion of the poetry of Joanna Baillie. It is enough to daunt the most confident. It is not a simple question of one school failing to appreciate another. The situation is much more disconcerting than that ; it involves the failure (and its converse) on the part of some trained and even sensitive critics to recognise any literary worth in works which, fundamentally, did actually embody the elements which they held to constitute such worth. The critics were not myopic or squint-eyed, but downright blind. They went astray in applying their own standards, in addition to failing to appreciate new ones. And the reason was just a difference of approach, a difference of method, which came between them and the real object. Examples of this are commonplaces in the history of criticism, and it applies to music and the visual arts as well as to literature. Can we attempt to analyse those factors which tend to vitiate the judging of contemporary literature ?

Sensibility differs in different ages more radically than we are sometimes aware, and an awareness of the nature of contemporary sensibility is indispensable in judging modern literature. We must be able to discount the appeal made to an overwrought mind by temporary factors playing unduly on the emotions. Such factors belong to an age as much as to individuals and are perhaps the greatest obstacle to the critic in assessing the work of his own day. An obvious example of this would be the temporary appeal of patriotic poetry at the beginning of a war or of hysterical " horror " poetry at the end. It was not easy to see in 1918 that Wilfred Owen was by far the best of the war poets, but as soon as the special type of sensibility evoked by the war had disappeared his pre-eminence was generally recognised. In Mr Middleton Murry's autobiography *Between Two Worlds* occurs this illuminating passage :

> In the previous number of *Rhythm* I had written a dithyrambic review of Mr James Stephens' book of poetry, *The Hill of Vision*. A poem in it which had, indeed, moved me deeply, called " The Lonely God," I had forthwith declared to be better than Milton : a dozen lines of it were worth the whole of *Endymion*. What had happened, quite simply, was that the poem *had* moved me, where modern poetry seldom did move me, and that I declared the fact in these ridiculous terms—setting it above *Paradise Lost*, which did not then move me, and *Endymion*, which I had never really read.

In this case an individual is concerned, but a whole age may make a very similar kind of error. The eighteenth century elevated many a poet of whom to-day few have heard above a poet like Donne, whom the age as a whole had " never really read." For certain temporary causes the critics were unnaturally sensitive to one kind of literature and unnaturally insensitive to another. And this is not a defect of any one age ; every age has its weaknesses and its blind spots, and a time when every kind of literature will be equally appreciated is inconceivable, if indeed it is desirable. Skelton is in favour to-day, but two hundred years ago he was execrated. Neither the favour which he enjoys at present nor the disfavour under which he so long laboured was due entirely to intrinsically literary reasons at all. The sensibility of the present age is unnaturally appreciative of Skelton. And almost every reaction and counter-reaction in literary taste points the same moral.

Another point to consider is that the critics of any one age are educated in the taste of the preceding age. When a twentieth century academic critic turns to verse, he generally writes in a nineteenth century idiom. As Wordsworth pointed out, the poet himself creates the taste by which he is to be judged ; it generally takes a generation or longer for this taste to be formed. So here is another factor which tends to confuse the judging of contemporary literature. And this explains, too, the unnatural impatience of many present-day poets with Victorian literary standards and traditions. They realise that these standards are formed on the basis of a previous age's achievement : they fail to realise that the standards are perfectly adequate when applied to work of a certain kind, with a certain function, although they are irrelevant to work with a different function altogether.

There is also such a thing as a quite irrational change in literary taste, which is apt to influence the critic at all points quite apart from his conscious attitude. How far such changes affect the fundamentals of literature is a debatable question, but that they concern every one of its accidentals cannot be questioned. A certain metre might be deemed " vulgar " by one generation while all other generations might find no fault of that kind with it whatever. Even definitions of such terms as " sentimental," " profound," " poetic," etc., are constantly changing. What is sentimental to a vicious degree to one age might appear restrained and classical to another.

An equally distorting factor is the tendency of any given generation to pride itself on producing work of historical importance and originating a highly significant new tradition. This leads to a judging of literature based entirely on this supposed historical standard and often to a complete abandonment of any adequate literary criterion. This attitude is particularly rife at the present day, when poets are praised for defining new attitudes, for breaking away from a certain tradition, for being in a certain movement, quite irrespective of the poetic value of their work. *The Waste Land*, for example, is frequently praised as poetry for quite irrelevant reasons. This is not to say that *The Waste Land* is not good poetry, but that the reasons often given for its being acclaimed good poetry are quite beside the point. The inability to distinguish between the *good* and the *important* is a frequent critical deficiency. We find it not only in discussion of contemporary work, but also very commonly in academic criticism of past literature — the type of criticism which puts *Gorboduc* above *Hamlet*, because while the latter was merely an experiment in an already established mode, the former was the first play of its kind. Undoubtedly works which are of historical importance deserve close study and are of considerable interest, but this does not mean that they are necessarily of any intrinsic value as literature. The historical critic is concerned with quite different values from those assessed by the purely literary critic. An attempt to take up a historical point of view in criticising contemporary work often leads to a complete lack of perspective which succeeding ages will at once detect and deride, and may also produce a confusion of values which will add greatly to the difficulty of the contemporary critic's already difficult task.

But can the critic find no anchor to prevent him from drifting on the tide of changing taste and muddled standards? There is the obvious safeguard of a fixed standard firmly adhered to and ruthlessly applied. That was the method of the early eighteenth century, and though it brought

JUDGING CONTEMPORARY LITERATURE 123

the critics a certain peace of mind in their activity
(which was satisfactorily counteracted by personal
animosity of the Pope *v.* Dennis variety) and a very
genuine insight in judging their own kind of work,
it narrowed their point of view so lamentably as
to make it quite impossible for them to judge
adequately anything written even in their own
language outside their own age. To-day we know
better than to apply rules and to speak of " kinds " :
have we not had over a hundred years of romantic
freedom to profit by ?

But have we profited ? Have we found any
more adequate method of judging contemporary
literature ? We have found out how to judge
literature impressionistically, to play the cultured
egoist and spin bookfulls of criticism out of our own
indulged emotions. Let us be quite clear concerning the value of this type of Romantic criticism.
It often results in products which are themselves
genuine literature ; many of the nineteenth century
essayists, working on these lines, have produced
pleasing literary work of the kind known as *belles-
lettres,* and it would be churlish as well as uncritical
to deny value to this type of writing as some of our
modern critics are inclined to do. But treated
simply as literary criticism their work is valueless.
When Hazlitt chats about Orlando Friscobaldo—

I can take mine ease in mine inn with Signor Orlando
Friscobaldo as the oldest acquaintance I have. Ben Jonson,
learned Chapman, Master Webster and Master Heywood
are there—

it is pleasant and readable but certainly not criticism. This is true, also, of such a passage as this from Lamb :

I confess for myself that (with no great delinquencies to answer for) I am glad for a season to take an airing beyond the diocese of the strict conscience—not to live always in the precincts of the law-courts—but now and then, for a dream-while or so, to imagine a world with no meddling restrictions —to get into recesses, whither the hunter cannot follow me—

> . . . Secret Shades
> Of woody Ida's inmost grove,
> While yet there was no fear of Jove.

I come back to my cage and my restraint the fresher and more healthy for it. I wear my shackles more contentedly for having respired the breath of an imaginary freedom. I do not know how it is with others, but I feel the better always for the perusal of one of Congreve's—nay, why should I not add even of Wycherley's—comedies.

It is no critical help to discourse smoothly about a character in a play as though he had an independent existence, or to prefix " Master " to the names of Webster and Heywood, neither does Lamb make a real contribution to criticism when he informs us of some personal facts of the kind quoted. Both these writers did produce some real criticism in addition to their personal essays, but their descendants are writing neither pleasing essays nor criticism of any value. To apply this egoistic method of criticism to contemporary writing, as so many writers are still doing, is the very height of literary folly. It is impossible to achieve by this method any adequate estimate of the work in consideration ; it is a simple shirking of the issue and generally implies a complete lack of real critical ability, indeed of any intellectual ability. Far from making any attempt to discount those factors which vitiate contemporary criticism, such a method deliberately surrenders to those factors, deliberately allows the writer to be influenced and prejudiced by those forces which have just been discussed. There are only too many examples of the sad mess such writers make in discussing contemporary poetry. Perhaps no one can be entirely successful in discussing the poetry of his own day, there is always something to blind the critic or distort his vision, but the personal essay type of criticism is the most patently inadequate and by its very nature is unfitted even to begin such a task.

So if eighteenth century rigour cannot provide the anchor, nineteenth century licence is even less successful. Where, then, are we to turn ? Can the " touchstone " theory of Matthew Arnold give us any help ? That is perhaps the most treacherous theory of all. It implies a view of literature which is fundamentally unsound—a view which regards the total literary achievement of a civilisation as something static, determined, both qualitatively and chronologically, so that we can take examples of great literature produced during a certain period of time and apply them as touchstones to literature of another period. As though there would be any point in judging a line like Hopkins'

And you were a liar O blue March day

by putting beside it

> In la sua volontade è nostra pace,

or in judging Eliot's lines

> Shall I say, I have gone at dusk through narrow streets
> And watched the smoke that rises from the pipes
> Of lonely men in shirt-sleeves, leaning out of windows? . . .

by setting it alongside

> Absent thee from felicity awhile,
> And in this harsh world draw thy breath in pain,
> To tell my story.

Such juxtapositions tell us exactly nothing. Not that there are no highest common factors to all great literature ; if the phrase " great literature " means anything at all these highest common factors must exist ; but this is not the way to bring them out. In any case, Arnold's criterion applies only to single lines and cannot be applied at all to complete works.

Arnold's touchstone method is due to an insufficiently organic view of literature, and in noting this we can discover at least a point of view—if nothing more precise—that will help the critic to achieve some sort of objectivity in judging contemporary literature. The critic must always bear in mind the *flexibility* of literature, its capability of infinite variety, its habit of throwing up quite new achievements which reflect back on the past and make us see all that has gone before in a new light at the same time as the new achievements themselves gain added significance from being viewed in relation to the body of previous writing. We cannot judge a line of Hopkins by comparing it with a line of Dante any more than we can judge a line of Dante by comparing it with a line of Hopkins. The quality and substance and merit of Dante's poetry are not fixed for all time, but change and grow richer as subsequent literature changes and develops, reflecting back new light on the past. It is as though a gem were set in an environment which was continually expanding and growing more brilliant, so that the gem itself took on new reflections and was seen in an ever-changing light, responding to its altering environment with a constantly enhanced glory.   So that in judging contemporary literature we cannot, for example, take the achievement of the previous four hundred years and extract from that a standard or a definition to apply to the ten years after the four hundredth. We must extract our standard or definition from all four hundred and ten years first before we are in a position to give adequate consideration to contemporary achievements.   This is all the more necessary at a time like the present when many new forms of literature are bewildering the critics, who are driven to take a standard from previous literature to apply to the present, instead of taking all literature, including that of their own day, in their view and deducing criteria accordingly.   This does not mean that the view of contemporary literature will necessarily be more favourable ; but it will be more understanding and therefore more just.

Further, the contemporary critic must be more than ordinarily careful to distinguish between absolute and historical value. In an age of self-conscious movements, when the clique and manifesto are much in evidence, cool-headedness regarding absolute literary value is rare. The tendency to a multiplicity of " schools " and the assessing of work solely with reference to such schools does not make for criticism which is likely to stand the test of time.

But what is this " absolute literary value " which we have been discussing ? This, of course, is the main problem, and it can only be solved by the individual critic. The highest common factor of great literature may be defined quite differently by different critics of equal sensitivity and experience, and others again may prefer not to define it at all. But a knowledge of it is possible and need not necessarily be accompanied by consistent definition. The conditions of such knowledge are difficult and exacting. It demands not only this organic view of literature already mentioned, but an insight into the nature and conditions of literary activity which can only come with wide and deep experience. The critic must know something of the relation of theory to practice throughout the course of literary history, he must be familiar with the manifold changes in taste and point of view which have occurred in the past and be able to correlate them to a view of the scope of literature as a whole. He must be able to view a contemporary work at once in isolation, purely on its own merits, and in its relation—

its complex and many-sided relation—to previous literature. And, perhaps most important of all, he must be able to distinguish clearly between the " universal " and the " particular " and note the presence or absence of one in the other. This distinction has reference to the one criterion of literary worth which cannot change and which is at the basis of all adequate critical theory from Aristotle onwards.

This is vague and shadowy advice for the critic who wishes to free himself from the snares that lie in wait for those who sit in judgment on contemporary literature. Yet what more can be said ? Perhaps this, that contemporary assessment can never be entirely adequate, and the greatest critic will leave some mistakes for posterity to laugh at. The best advice can only be negative : avoid rules, avoid egoistic impressionism, avoid treating literature as a matter of personal " purgation " for the writer, avoid seeking a false *justification* for writing which has no objective value. Ultimately there is no justification for literature which is not a literary one—and this fact is not so obvious as it sounds, if we are to judge from the number of critics who ignore it.

At all events, the judging of contemporary literature is not a task for the dilettante or the gossip writer or the armchair critic. Methods which may be profitable or at least interesting in discussing aspects of past literature are neither when employed in discussing the work of the critic's own day.

R

Contemporary criticism is a serious and difficult business. One of the best ways of learning to appreciate its difficulty and at the same time helping oneself to see into the nature of real criticism is to study the bad " misses " of the great critics of the past. That will indicate more clearly than anything the kind of trap that is always awaiting the critic and perhaps give him a greater sense of responsibility. For most contemporary criticism shows neither responsibility nor humility, and without these two virtues no critical work of any worth can be achieved.

February, 1936.

LITERATURE AND BELIEF

IT is a pertinent question whether literature can use as its material the facts of life—intellectual, emotional, psychological, as well as physical—without making use also of an extraneous non-literary background in which to place them and determine their relations. Do such facts possess any quite independent determinable *qualities* of their own, or do they come to possess qualities and values only in so far as we impose upon them standards which are derived from other sources? It may be argued that no other sources exist, and it is of course true that ultimately all standards must be drawn from the facts of experience in one of its aspects ; but this argument is irrelevant if by " other sources " we refer to a difference in time rather than in essential origin. A religious tradition may derive from an original experience or series of experiences which are undoubted " facts of life," yet such a tradition may be used as a background to a treatment of contemporary facts to which it owes nothing. And this applies not only to a religious tradition, but equally to the assumptions of an age or a civilisation. A mediæval lyric, for example, treats its theme in the light of the values of mediæval Christendom, while in the

eighteenth century a poet like, say, Prior takes for
granted another set of values, equally comprehensive,
which forms a permanent background to the slightest
piece of verse he writes. There is no need to
multiply examples of different backgrounds implied
in the literary work of different ages : a study of
literary history shows at once that the experience
which is the theme of any given composition is
not allowed to define its own significance but draws
on a background of belief to give it objectivity and
intelligibility.

The critic is seldom troubled about this because
he is rarely concerned to enquire whether experience
has native, inherent quality *sui generis* which will
justify the literary artist in endeavouring to portray
it in isolation and to ignore anything that might
suggest a scale of values which has its origin elsewhere. Yet the question is surely a fundamental
one, since if such quality exists it is the duty of
literature to concern itself with it to the exclusion
of all else. The practice in the past is clear enough :
in all previous ages the implications of literature
were fully seen only when the fact described or
expressed had been related to a common body of
belief. How else could the writer establish contact
with his public at all ? How could he make any
normative comment or illustration if there was not
a universally accepted higher scale of values with
reference to which he could make his points ? How
could he use an effective symbolism without drawing
on a common stock of material with an emotional

value that could be depended on? What could be his excuse for writing at all if it was not contained by implication in the system of thought of the age in which he wrote? Consider the problem of a poet endeavouring to express his feeling on a particular occasion—say, on viewing a moonlit landscape—without having any other belief, or assuming in his readers any other belief, than what that experience called into being. Could he produce a work of any objectivity at all?

That is really what the question becomes—it resolves itself into a consideration of the relation of belief (or tradition) to objectivity, self-contained intelligibility, in art. Obviously the poet in the condition just postulated could write *something*, but whether that something could convey any sense of the nature or value of his experience to any other person is quite another matter. To what extent would the work contain its meaning in itself? It could of course be given meaning by explanation embodied in a footnote or appendix or some such help, but that is only to say that the writer has failed to make his poem an adequate vehicle of expression. Further, such explanation would probably have to make use of this background of belief which the poet rejected in the work itself.

The function of comparison, direct or implied, is more important in literature than is generally realised. We grasp the unknown through its being put in relation to the known, and no new fact or experience can have value for us until we see it with reference to the body of accepted fact which is part tradition, part past experience. This is particularly so in literature (as distinct from " scientific " writing) whose method is more deliberately evocative and associational than other forms of communication. Thus a poet gives us his sense of the value of a new experience by reference to other values which we accept. Those other values may in time be supplanted by those very new values whose nature we grasp only when they are expressed in terms of the old, but they are nevertheless of prime importance in establishing the initial contact between writer and reader. The new values in " nature " that the Romantic movement brought were originally expressed in terms of a common belief and common standards which soon after passed away. The greatest revolutions in " taste " and æsthetic habits were brought about by setting the new ideas against a background of general belief, and it was thus that they were made intelligible. And if this is true of the revolutionary writer, it is certainly true of the writer who interprets the accepted outlook of an age to itself.

So while the " fact itself " may exist absolutely, in its capacity for expression it exists only with reference to irrelevant belief. Experience has " quality " in that given aspects of it have power to move, to rouse to a sense of significance ; but to make this quality objectively intelligible the writer must depend on factors which certainly have no immediate connection with the theme he is treating, however probable an ultimate [1] connection may appear. A limited kind of communication would, indeed, be possible if the writer confined himself to reference to values of a similar kind ; if, for example, in describing our hypothetical moonlit scene he referred—directly or symbolically or in any of the numerous indirect ways of reference open to him—to other experiences of a similar kind and to æsthetic values as known and understood. But such writing must at best be very thin and will always tend to be repetitive in form and circular in argument. To link up a given experience to the values of life as a whole (including moral values), which surely is the aim of the true literary artist, there is necessary a convenient means of transition from the particular instance to the sum of experience, and such a means is provided by a scheme of things common to the artist and his public. Even if a full expression of the "fact itself" were possible, it is doubtful whether it would have any value left in the isolation which strict relevance to the particular instance—or even to the particular *kind* of experience—demands.

That is why artists always work within a civilisation and an accepted scheme of things. It is only thus that they are able to pierce through the "particular" to the "universal" and establish intelligible contact with reality. I stress *intelligible* contact, because personal contact merely is of no

[1] Ultimate in the temporal sense, as indicated earlier.

general value, having significance only for the writer himself. Reality schematised, however arbitrarily or stupidly, is none the less reality, and the schematisation—of values more than of phenomena —gives the man of letters that background of allusion and reference, that store-house of comparison and symbolism, that source of illustration and illumination, without which higher forms of literary expression are unattainable.

The reliance on such a background of belief must not be taken to imply lack of an individual approach. Both Dante and Milton had very individual ways of looking at life, yet their work was only possible in the framework they chose. Dante is perhaps the most extreme case of a writer working within a civilisation ; the whole mediæval scheme of thought is implied, and parts are quite explicit, in the *Divina Commedia*. Milton took less for granted and put a more personal interpretation on what he did accept, yet seventeenth century Protestant civilisation, in its secular as well as its religious aspect, informs his work throughout.

The important point is not so much that the poet should have a personal belief as that he should share a body of belief with his public. Otherwise adequate communication cannot be established. It is not the poet's duty to create a symbolism from his own consciousness or form a body of allusion out of his own private experience ; such literary inbreeding has many and obvious dangers ; his function is rather to express his own message by symbolism and allusion based on what is known and accepted by his public. It is no illumination to illustrate the unknown by the equally unknown. One might compare the activity of the literary artist to that of the keeper of a scrap-book, who pastes his scraps on to the stiff pages of the book. He must have a background on which to fit his scraps, otherwise he can do nothing with them ; they flutter to the ground unsupported. So the writer must have a background on which to paste his ideas, something that will hold them together and define their relations. No writer can provide purely out of his consciousness at once scraps and scrap-book ; he has done his duty as an artist when he has provided the former and pasted them on the pages provided by his age in the most satisfying arrangement. It is no use protesting that this means the enslavement of the writer. Literary communication is possible in no other way, and the true literary artist will find in the conditions of his activity opportunity rather than embarrassment.

It may be asked why, if such are the conditions of literary communication, writers are intelligible to other ages than their own. How can we appreciate work done within a tradition which is now dead ? The answer is twofold. In the first place, the reader who has not the knowledge to enable him to understand the dead tradition will get very much less out of the work than he imagines. It is not generally realised how completely *wrong*

s

(if not merely blank) the response of the intelligent but ignorant reader must be to, say, Dante or Milton, or the Greek and Latin classics. If the reader who knows nothing of Greek values and the Greek scheme of things gets anything out of Greek literature it is not because that literature has communicated to him what its authors intended it to communicate, but because he brings to his reading a preconceived set of emotional values and associations (generally highly " romantic ") drawn from his other reading which enables him to get a vague, undefined sentimental pleasure whose connection with the actual work read has very little reality. It is time critics faced up to this question of the appreciation of literature written in a dead tradition, and realised how difficult it is and how rarely it is attained. The approach to such literature is more often than not purely sentimental, that is to say, all the reader does is to look out for dimly perceived emotional contacts which he uses in order to induce an almost autobiographical reverie by means of association and substitution. Snobbish though it may sound, it is none the less true that genuine appreciation of a past literature is impossible without a great deal of knowledge and—more important—the insight which such knowledge brings.

There is a second point. This need of knowledge is to some extent counterbalanced by the fact that writers working within a framework unconsciously reveal that framework and induce the reader to take it for granted without quite realising what he is doing. It is thus that much past work becomes intelligible to us. The whole background of belief behind a writer and the contemporary public he wrote for is insinuated into our minds as we read, so that, while our conscious selves might angrily repudiate it, while we read we accept it and allow the author to establish communication by means of it. We rarely realise how constantly we enter a state of " willing suspension of disbelief " in order to appreciate the significance of a writer. Such a mood is quite different from the scholar's deliberate assumption of a foreign standpoint a knowledge of which he has acquired through study ; it emanates from the work itself and it alone makes it possible —though by no means inevitable—for the reader who is not scholar enough to add the background himself nevertheless to have some genuine appreciation of work written in an outgrown tradition. So the answer to the question : " How can we appreciate literature produced within a scheme of things that has passed away ? " is firstly, that very often we do not appreciate it when we think we do, and, secondly, that literature has the power to communicate its own assumptions which sometimes enables us to come into direct contact with the spirit of a dead civilisation.

But we must not assume that because literature can to some extent communicate its own assumptions when these belong to the age of the author it can do so if the assumptions are entirely personal and belong to the author alone. A writer who makes use of no tradition, no common background of belief, will find it difficult to make contact at any time. The state of literature to-day provides an interesting example of what can happen when, for the first time, all community of ideas has been abandoned. " Most great literature," writes Mr Day Lewis in his stimulating essay *Revolution in Writing*, " has a coherent philosophy at the back of it : to English literature, from the mystery plays to Wordsworth, the Christian philosophy has been a background—and often the backbone too. But for the last 100 years this background has been disintegrating, till now nothing remains of it but a few faded tatters stitched together with every variety of pseudo-scientific, mystico-emotional, liberal-humanist material." It is impossible to deny the general truth of Mr Lewis's statement. What exactly are its implications ?

If no attempt to deal with reality in literature can be successful without an accepted schematisation of values, then the contemporary writer must be faced with an almost impossible task. It is primarily a question of communication and objectivity, and it is precisely in these two respects that modern literature is least successful. That the charge of incomprehensibility is the main one brought by " conservative " critics against present-day writers is no coincidence ; it is due to the fact that contact between artist and public is becoming less and less possible in direct proportion to the disappearance of a common background of belief. That, as Dr Leavis has pointed out, is the significance of *The Waste Land*. This poem shows what happens when the poet has to create his own mythology, his own terms of reference, his own store-house of symbolism. There are more glaring examples than *The Waste Land*. A glance through any of the numerous anthologies of contemporary verse that have recently appeared will show poets, divorced from all tradition, accepting no discoverable scheme of values, struggling to express their reactions to different experiences in terms purely of their own consciousness. The great progress of psycho-analysis in recent times has had the influence on literature that it has had because psycho-analysis suggested a method of tapping individual consciousness while completely ignoring other values.

This is a point worth considering. The present relation of psychology to literature has only been made possible by the decay of uniform belief. Free association, attempts at deliberate exploitation of the subconscious for its own sake, and other similar devices so common in contemporary writing, are alternative methods of expression to the traditional one of utilising a common background. Writers are being driven more and more to isolated introspection as a means of suggesting types of emotion and even trains of thought. No longer concerned to link up their experiences with the common experience of men, they are forced to treat of unevaluated aspects of consciousness. This does not mean simply that they lay bare their own reactions without distinguishing between them and leave it to the reader to evaluate ; such an achievement is in itself considerable and is compatible with the production of great literature ; it means that most often *expression* is not attained at all, that nothing is laid bare, that the works have no objective value whatever. The acceptance of a background of belief does not mean that the writer is bound to express the values which those beliefs imply. It means that, there being common ground on which he can meet his readers, there are points of reference on whose effectiveness he can count in his method of expression. It is largely a matter of technique, of vocabulary even. To take some crude examples, words like " God," " duty," " society," "noble," " nature," have meaning only with reference to some schematisation of belief, and change with the differing assumptions of different ages. But when it is known that men are bound by no community of ideas, when there is no orthodoxy and no heterodoxy, when men are split up into groups consisting sometimes of no more than one, such words lack precision of meaning, often lack all meaning. And if this is true of single words, it is just as true and much more portentous in the case of larger units of expression and of modes of writing in general.

It is not surprising, therefore, that both the technique and the function of literature is changing before our eyes. A single factor is behind both these changes. The disappearance of ground

common to writer and public has put a gap
between the two quite different in kind from any
barrier that may have existed in the past. It
is not merely that, to quote Mr Lewis again,
" the poet realizes that he is no longer popular :
accordingly he has no incentive to gild his poetry
with the stuff of entertainment : he is deprived of
that feeling of writing for a wide audience which
understood his language ; and therefore he begins
to write for the tiny circle of people with whom
he is in contact, and his poetry sounds to outsiders
—what in fact it is—the private language of personal
friends." There are more fundamental elements
in the situation than that. Poets are driven to
write for those friends with whom they have a
scheme of things in common because it is only
with them that literary communication is possible.
But poets of this kind represent only one type of
contemporary writer, and a type that is in the
minority. The majority have changed more drastic-
ally than by merely narrowing their public. They
have become their own public, and forged a medium
of expression out of their private beliefs and associations so that the real implications of their work are
intelligible only to themselves. This is the cause of
that " private symbolism " that justly causes concern
to so many critics.

What aggravates the situation is that in the face
of this great change in the nature of literary activity,
those who profess to understand and appreciate
the " new literature " do not as a rule understand

it and appreciate it on its merits, for what it is. They nearly always approach it in the same sentimental uncritical way in which so many people approach the literature of a past age, seeking for points of emotional contact, deceiving themselves into connecting a chance phrase or even word with some past experience of their own. That is often the way in which people of no musical education listen to music—by forcing themselves to connect some melody with some particular pleasant landscape they have known or some moving incident, etc., so that they can sit back bathed in warm expansive emotion while the music is being played, and imagine that they are appreciating it as music. It is easy to express appreciation of modern poetry if it is approached in this sentimental manner, but such appreciation is of little value and certainly is no test of literary worth. A just sense of the nature of much contemporary writing is rarely found in the enthusiastic apologies for modern literature which appear so often.

The technique employed by the writers who have severed themselves from all community of belief—not always deliberately, but just because community of belief has ceased to exist—is often a development of methods used by those who were not yet influenced by the disintegration of the background. The influences behind the modern poets, from the French Symbolists to Joyce's *Ulysses* and *Work in Progress*, have in themselves no necessary connection with this writing out of the individual consciousness.

The Joycean technique which has been so influential on the " free-association " methods of present-day writers is adaptable to other purposes as well. But the writers have exploited this, as they have exploited psycho-analysis, in their endeavour to find methods of writing compatible with their situation. One must be careful, therefore, to distinguish between formal aspects of technique and the use to which the technique is put. Failure to keep this distinction in mind is another deficiency in many of the critics.

The result of the lack of a community of positive ideas has been to effect a real change in the nature of literary activity. That this has seriously interfered with the objectivity—the capacity for objective expression—of the literary medium cannot be doubted. It is more difficult to decide on the value of literature produced under such conditions. Perhaps in the future, when the intellectual and other movements of the present day will be seen in adequate perspective, it will be possible for the reader to reconstruct the mental background of present-day writers for himself and so gain a new appreciation of their work. We who are contemporaries must either be content with the sentimental approach discussed above, which does indeed yield appreciation of a kind, or else resolve to make a thorough biographical study of every new author we read, noting particularly the influences in his mental environment, so that we may be enabled to establish contact with his scheme of things and so get the full implications of his work. But perhaps the situation is not as bad as that. These arguments, after all, admittedly put the case at its most extreme, and there are many intermediate stages where, with a little effort, real understanding is still possible. There is in fact some background of belief extant—in matters of social morality, perhaps, and intellectual honesty ; or is this the beginning of a new background rather than the end of the old ?—and those who know how to avail themselves of its help in the field of expression can be genuinely successful in certain spheres of literary communication. In any case present conditions must by their very nature be temporary ; that they have lasted so long at all is probably due to the war. It may be undue optimism, but some profess to see a growing community of belief at least among not inconsiderable groups, a common background based on the finer elements of humanism combined with a new attitude to society and its problems. We cannot rush the process ; it must come naturally or not at all. Meanwhile the situation is both interesting and instructive to the literary critic.

March, 1936.